HEALING WITH CRYSTALS

D0064174

This series introduces a wide range of healing techniques that can be used either independently or as a complement to traditional medical treatment. Most of the techniques included in the series can be learnt and practised alone, and each encourages a degree of self-reliance, offering the tools needed to achieve and maintain an optimum state of health.

Each title opens with information on the history and principles of the technique and goes on to offer practical and straightforward guidance on ways in which it can be applied, with diagrams and case studies where appropriate. Please note that readers are advised to seek professional guidance for serious ailments, and to make use of the list of practitioners for further guidance. Many of the techniques in this series are taught in workshops and adult education classes; all of the titles are written by professional practitioners with many years of experience and proven track records.

AVAILABLE IN THIS SERIES

Healing with Ayurveda — Angela Hope-Murray and
    Tony Pickup
Healing with Colour — Helen Graham
Healing with Essential Oils — Nicola Naylor
Healing with Herbs — Judith Hoad
Healing with Homeopathy — Peter Chappell and
    David Andrews
Healing with Meditation — Doriel Hall
Healing with Osteopathy — Peta Sneddon and Paolo Coseschi
Healing with Reflexology — Rosalind Oxenford
Healing with Shiatsu — Catherine Sutton

FORTHCOMING TITLES IN THIS SERIES
Healing with Flower Essences
Healing with Nutritional Therapy

Healing with Crystals

JACQUIE BURGESS

Gill & Macmillan

Gill & Macmillan Ltd
Goldenbridge
Dublin 8
with associated companies throughout the world
© Jacquie Burgess 1997
0 7171 2488 6
Series editor: Tessa Strickland
Series copy editor: Pamela Dix
Illustrations by Design Image, Dublin
Index compiled by Helen Litton
Original text design by Identikit Design Consultants, Dublin
Print origination by Carole Lynch
Printed by ColourBooks Ltd, Dublin

This book is typeset in 10/15 pt Bembo.

All rights reserved. No part of this publication may be copied,
reproduced or transmitted in any form or by any means,
without permission of the publishers.

A catalogue record is available for this book from
the British Library.

1 3 5 4 2

Contents

TO MY PARENTS CHRIS AND BRIDGET, WITH LOVE

This is a book I badly wanted to write, especially since I began teaching crystal healing in Ireland. I have met many remarkable men and women who have generously brought their openness, talent and sensitivity to the workshops. It is largely due to their inspiration, as well as to the courage and experiences of my private clients, that this book exists.

CHAPTER ONE

What is Crystal Healing and How Does it Work?

T he patient was a middle-aged professional with a
history of migraine attacks dating back to his teens.
The headaches seemed resistant to most orthodox
forms of treatment, so his usual approach to an attack was
to take to his bed and try to sleep until the pain went away
— typically in about twenty-four hours. He did not
believe in crystal therapy, having instead a perception of
crystals as a fashion accessory favoured by the wilder
fringes of the New Age movement.

This man might have ended his days without
changing his opinion if he had not been stricken by a
migraine while visiting my London flat. It began with
scintillations and blanks in his field of vision, progressing
to nausea and a blinding headache. He was so thoroughly
miserable that I asked him if he would like a crystal
treatment. I was given the sort of look familiar to a witch-
doctor called to treat a European in the terminal stage of
Ebola: the patient doesn't think the witch-doctor can help
him, but he's so desperate he'll try anything. My patient
obediently lay down on my treatment couch, sighed and
closed his eyes. He was by now in so much pain he wasn't
even curious about what I might be doing.

What I was in fact doing was laying a grid of small
quartz crystal points on and around his body. The primary
symptom of migraine is severe headache triggered by
dilation of the blood-vessels servicing the brain, but in
many instances other organs are involved — notably the

gall-bladder or liver and sometimes even the kidneys. I
used the crystals to try to bring balance to them all. The
head received special treatment, with a small fluorite
crystal placed on the brow and flat pieces of jade laid on
the closed eyes.

'How are you feeling now?' I asked when I'd
completed the layout. He groaned, which I took to mean
no improvement.

Although he hadn't asked, I began to explain what
I was trying to do — I'm a great believer in keeping the
patient informed. A few minutes into the explanation
my patient suddenly sat bolt upright, sending the crystals
flying.

'Good God!' he exclaimed. 'It's gone!'

'The headache?' I asked hopefully.

'The headache, the nausea, the eye trouble —
everything. It's incredible. One minute it was there, the
next minute it all stopped. It was like switching off a light.'

Crystals are wonderful tools for balancing energy in
our bodies, our minds, our emotions and our
environment. Although they don't always work in the
spectacular fashion I've just described — even for
migraine — their unique properties make them invaluable
in a therapeutic context across a broad spectrum of
ailments. Crystals have certainly changed my own life.
Since I began working with them, more than ten years
ago, my life has undergone a series of personal and
professional transformations that took me from the world
of publishing to my own therapy practice, from single life
to married bliss, from the heart of London to the depths
of County Carlow.

Of course everything changes — even the atoms of
our bodies are ninety-nine per cent recycled within twelve

months. Atoms that were part of you may now be in me. But despite knowing this in theory, I believed in the fixed nature of my personal reality. And so I could not fully receive the powerful medicine of life already in me.

Crystal healing is the use of crystals on or around the body to effect beneficial changes and redress imbalances. Crystals boost low energy; screen out damaging energy; release stagnant or blocked energy; and transform destructive patterns. This approach to health is based on the view that all life is made up of energy and the physical body is a microcosm reflecting the macrocosm of the universe. Our planet and, ultimately, the universe, exists as a perpetual dance of balancing forces. The air we breathe, the heat and light of the sun, water and food, are all energies on which we depend for life. As organisms we are finely balanced to take in, store, transform and transmit energy. So if something in our personal energy system or in the balance of our environment breaks down, the balance of life-supporting functions is impaired and we can spiral into a destructive pattern of disease.

LIFE FORCE

According to scientists, we are surrounded by a sea of radiation. Most of it is generated by the sun — some reaches us from outer space. These two sources combine with energies produced by the earth itself and by humanity in the form of radio and television broadcasts, electricity supply and so forth. All of it comes together to form an energy soup of background radiation against which every activity on earth takes place. This energy soup is measurable using modern instruments, but was, in fact, suspected by ancient civilisations long before such measuring equipment was developed. Some of them even recognised that aspects of this radiation — notably those wavelengths generated by the sun — are the ultimate driving force behind all life on our planet.

The energy now being measured by scientists is the very same energy which the vedic tradition refers to as *prana*, called *chi* in China, and *ki* in Japan. I will refer to it as life force since that's exactly what it is. Life force is expressed differently on different levels of reality: in becoming matter it affects all physical functions, but the same life force is also the pure consciousness of eastern spiritual aspiration. So when we are able to experience a sense of bliss, an all-pervading peace, love, at-one-ment, we touch the spiritual aspect of the life force and a return to wholeness and a connectedness with all that is.

The healing qualities of the life force are most graphically demonstrated in the Chinese acupuncture system, which treats the body by balancing the flow of *chi* energy passing through it. Ayurvedic medicine utilises *prana* to balance the system in a similar way. The more life force we can absorb and circulate on all levels, the more balanced, healthy and in-tune we become. The intention in crystal healing is to transform the spiritual, 'unmanifest', life force into forms of energy that we can actually use.

Energy moves in mysterious ways, however. Every thought we have affects energy, often building complex patterns that profoundly influence who we are and how we experience life. And since everybody has an energy field, we can affect our health by changing our thoughts. Everyone has experienced the influence of sadness, anger, sorrow or joy on their well-being. Repeated exposure to negative thoughts, whether our own or another's, can lead to depression and physical disease, while experience of loving kindness and beauty can soothe, inspire and heal.

Health is also affected by changes in the energy field that surrounds our bodies. We are influenced from outside by what is happening in our environment and the energy states of the people in it. It is both the chicken and the egg: thought influences energy and energy influences thought. But we have the power to choose how we respond and as such to influence our health. Optimum health depends on cooperation with life's natural balance. This is not easy, since it means living as consciously and as sensitively as possible, reconnecting with our real selves.

Crystal healing takes an essentially holistic approach, which means that the whole picture of the patient — lifestyle, attitudes, state of mind, environment — is taken into account. It is a therapy that aims to restore the balance and well-being of the whole person. It works by assisting us to tune in to the rhythms of life, to respect creation, to balance the forces and influences that play through our lives, releasing attitudes and habits which no longer serve us.

CRYSTAL ENERGY AND HOW IT WORKS

Crystals were used in the earliest shamanic rites as tools for initiation and healing, for talismans, for prophesy and for mystical contemplation. Today, they are no less important as vital components in our scientific technology. But alongside this technology, increasing numbers of people are reconsecrating crystals once more to their ancient sacred functions.

In our high-tech world, it is hard to believe how dramatically crystals influence our lives. We inhabit a planet that is largely made up of crystals and we live in buildings made possible by crystals. Natural stone is crystalline in structure, as are most artificial building materials. Even the cement that binds them depends on crystal growth to harden. Crystals underpin a huge amount of the technology, science and medicine on which our civilisation depends. Without crystals we would have no micro computers, modern telecommunications equipment or laser surgery. As Ian Mercer says in an excellent introduction to the subject:

> You use people's knowledge and control of the ways that crystals behave whenever you cross bridges, enjoy sweets, watch TV, travel by train, car or plane, paint the front door, hold a cup, ring home, drill for oil and look at the time.

Crystals have played an important role in orthodox medicine throughout history and continue to do so today. One typical example is kunzite — a variety of the crystal group spodumene — which has become the prime source of lithium. Lithium, when administered as lithium carbonate (a white powder), is an important drug in the prevention and treatment of manic depression. Lithium also played a role in one of the most important discoveries of the twentieth century. In 1932, John D. Cockcroft and Ernest Walton bombarded lithium with electrically accelerated protons and actually transformed it into another element. Transmutation is now a common process because of the availability of powerful particle accelerators and nuclear reactors. More than 1,500 radioisotopes have been synthesised, many of which have valuable medical and industrial uses. The alchemist's miracle is possible today — all because of processes involving crystals.

You don't need a particle accelerator, however, to demonstrate the more interesting properties of crystal. If you strike one end of a quartz crystal point in a darkened room, you will see a brief flash of light at the other. The light is, in fact, an electrical spark. What has happened is that the crystal transformed kinetic energy (the force of the blow) into electrical energy (the spark). The whole process is known technically as the piezo-electric effect — something that powers most cigarette lighters today.

Closely associated with the piezo-electric effect is the pyro-electric effect, another fascinating physical property of crystals. To demonstrate it, all you need to do is throw the right sort of crystal — tourmaline is a good choice — into the hot embers of a small wood or turf fire. As the crystal heats up, it first attracts then suddenly repels the ashes, due to a build-up of electrical charges on its surface.

Perhaps the most pleasing demonstration of a crystal's physical properties requires no tools at all. Shine a white light through a coloured crystal and coloured light comes out. This effect is so commonplace we seldom stop to consider what a miracle it is. In fact, the process is extraordinarily complex. The colour of light is directly related to its wavelength. Impurities in a crystal cause it to absorb certain frequencies of (white) light. Our eyes then pick up only the wavelengths not absorbed. The absorbed light gives the crystal its colour. The remaining wavelength determines the precise hue of the light that emerges. You can demonstrate this simply by hanging a crystal in your window or holding it up to the sun.

Some years ago, scientists experimenting with crystals discovered that if you squeezed them, they released a few electrons. Once you released the pressure and the crystal went back to its original shape, it absorbed the missing

electrons from the air around it. The scientists began to
wonder if it might be possible to reverse this process. In
other words, would a crystal expand if you forced it to
take in additional electrons and return to normal when
you switched off the electron stream?

The idea was easy to test experimentally. An electron
stream is only an electrical current. So they attached
electrodes to a piece of crystal, turned on the power and
made their measurements. The crystal did indeed expand
while the current was on and contracted back to its
original size when the current was switched off. We are
talking about tiny movements here — vibrations that
cannot be seen with the naked eye. But the thing about
crystal is that when you feed in a measured amount of
electricity, the degree of vibration it produces is absolutely
constant. If there is any variation at all, it is so small that
for all practical purposes it can be discounted.

This may not sound like a particularly important
discovery, but it is. The utter reliability of a crystal's
vibrations make it ideal as the heart of radio and television
sets, radar installations, computer systems — anywhere
where there is a need for accurate frequency control.
You may be wearing an example of this use of crystal
on your wrist right now.

So it is clear that on one level at least, the prime
characteristic of crystals is that of energy transformation —
the energy put into the crystal is not always and not
necessarily the same energy that comes out. The use of
crystal in optics and laser technology indicates an
additional talent for focusing and transmitting energy.
Crystals in computers also store energy.

The question is, do these proven properties operate
on more subtle levels, as ancient peoples believed? Many

modern experts think they do. In his book *Cosmic Crystals,* Ra Bonewitz differentiates between mundane and spiritual crystal effects. In the former category he places all those things we've just been discussing — the measurable effects of kinetic energy, electricity and so on. In the category of spiritual effects, he places energies like thought, will, healing, etc., that cannot be measured mechanically, but can certainly be *experienced.*

Bonewitz claims that the mundane properties of crystals are paralleled by spiritual attributions; an observation confirmed by crystal practitioners. Quartz, the most widely used crystal, transforms, focuses, amplifies, transmits and stores subtle energies as effectively as electricity.

THE SPIRITUAL PROPERTIES OF CRYSTALS

Clear quartz amplifies right brain function, which influences intuitive, feeling perceptions — so working with crystals can increase your intuition. You may experience increased awareness. You may develop a greater sensitivity to colours, sounds and energy flows in and around your body. You may discover you are psychic or telepathic. These are exciting developments, yet they are experienced by crystal practitioners sufficiently often to be an established, experiential fact.

Quartz also has the ability to transform an imbalanced energy field. So when you feel stressed, the crystal will move your energy back into balance and revitalise you. Quartz transmits life force throughout the human energy system, bringing healing and balance. Crystals are ideal for focusing your thoughts and receiving energy, a valuable part of meditation and healing practice. The clarity of quartz crystal makes it a perfect transmitter and amplifier of colour in healing. Finally, experience shows that quartz has the ability to store a thought form, which means that you can programme it for a specific purpose. Crystals can also help your meditation to reach for other levels of experience and to glimpse a little more of spiritual reality.

Apart from quartz, many others minerals display healing properties. The glorious spectrum of colours found in crystals is also of significance, since colours vibrate at differing rates. A violet amethyst vibrates at an extraordinary 750 trillions per second, while red ruby vibrates at the rate of 460 trillions per second. Many different crystals are described in the Directory, where the most popular stones are listed along with a guide to their traditional attributions.

Sensitivity is of vital importance for the effective crystal healer. Not only does each patient have his or her own personality, temperament and life experience, but each crystal also has its own unique character. This means that two similar-sized quartz points may be suitable for quite different types of work. It is the sensitivity and experience of the healer that determines the most appropriate way to work.

Healing with crystals is clearly not like using a cookbook. The physical ailment manifested is often not the root of the disease; one of the reasons crystals can be so helpful is that by re-balancing energy fields they can assist the patient's own body/mind healing process. Different patients with the same condition may require a different approach and may very well respond differently to the same crystals, depending on constitution, temperament and environment. Added to which, crystals respond to other crystals in a wide variety of ways. The healer's energy, the patient's energy and the crystal's energy all interact. These factors need to be considered with care in using crystals for healing.

CHAPTER TWO

The Origins of Crystal Healing

Crystals have been revered as sacred since earliest times. They were used for divining the hidden meaning of events, for travelling in non-ordinary reality and for healing the sick. They were believed by Native Americans to be gifts from the star people and their powers were highly respected. For an understanding of these ancient beliefs we can turn to still active shamanic traditions.

Michael Harner relates, in his book *The Way of the Shaman*, a fascinating experience he had many years ago with the Coast Miwok of California. He observed the 'waking' of a very large quartz crystal. The ceremony involved the tribe shaman striking the base of the crystal against a specific rock just off the coast. The tribe believed it to be a highly dangerous operation — if the crystal were smashed it would cause the end of the world. When Harner mentioned the ceremony to a well-known physicist, he was told that smashing such a large crystal might have ended the shaman's world, since the electrical energy released could easily have killed him.

In his standard work *Shamanism*, the anthropologist Mircea Eliade cites many examples from the Malay Peninsula, Australia and South America of quartz being used to initiate shamans into their full powers. The South American Cobeno shaman introduces rock crystals into the novice's head, where it is believed they replace his brain and give him his 'strength'. Among the Australian Aborigine peoples, initiation might involve abrading the skin with crystals or inserting small crystals under it. The crystals that play such an important part in these initiations are believed to originate from the sky. The Supreme Being, Baiame, throws crystal fragments down to earth from his clear crystal throne. The Negritos of the Malay Peninsula believe their magic crystals have a similar celestial origin.

Among the Sea Dyak of North Borneo, the shaman depends on quartz crystals, batu ilau, 'the stones of light' to help discover the patient's soul, for illness is due to loss of soul and the shaman's job is to retrieve it. The patient's body is rubbed with the sacred stones while the tribe chants and the shaman dances himself into trance. The best shamans also gazed into clear crystals to see past, present and future. This is the origin of our psychic's crystal ball.

CRYSTAL GAZING

Divining crystals were widely used among the Cherokee people. In his book *Secret Native American Pathways*, Thomas E. Mails is told by a Cherokee, Archie Sam, of putting a crystal in a running stream and watching the pictures that formed in the water running over the stone's surface. To discover the cause of an illness, the crystals were warmed over a fire and laid on the body. The shaman then looked 'through' the crystals to find the origin of the illness. The crystal that held the picture would then be placed in the sun, where it would reveal more about the illness and insights into effecting a cure. The shaman would also rub warmed crystals rapidly between his palms to give them strong vibrations before placing them on a painful part of the patient's body. The energy from the stones was so powerful that the entire body would shake violently before the patient became free of pain.

Many European country folk traditions involved crystals. In Scotland, cattle were given water that had been poured over crystals to drink. Crystals were also used as a protection for cattle in Ireland and to charm away vermin. Stones with markings in them like trees and mosses (dendrites such as moss agate) were especially associated with good fortune in crop growing and farming.

It is not only in the shamanic traditions, though, where we find evidence of the early use of crystals. Ancient vedic texts from India contain detailed metaphysical information about gemstones and their beneficial effects on the astrological chart. The texts go on to describe the talismanic powers of crystals, with warnings given of the dangers of inauspicious and poor-quality stones.

CRYSTALS IN THE SCRIPTURES

The Bible confirms that the ancient world set great store by crystals. In the New Testament, the rebuilt Jerusalem had gemstones placed in its foundations. The influence of the heavens was a vital part of healing in the Hebraic tradition, and in the Old Testament reference to Aaron's breastplate, both astrology and gem stones are combined. The stones of this garment allowed the priest to communicate with angels. There has been much speculation as to the exact stones incorporated into the breastplate, but what we do know is that such an artifact would have acted to enhance priestly intuition and strengthen his energy field. Isadore Kosminsky gives a detailed account of the probable stones used, their significance and meaning, in his classic text *The Magic and Science of Jewels and Stones*.

King Solomon was supposed to have worn a ring made of the four stones given to him by the four angels of Earth, Air, Fire and Water, showing his power over the

HEBREW NAME	MODERN NAME	EQUIVALENT ZODIAC SIGN
1 Odem	Red Hematite	Aries
2 Pitdah	Emerald	Taurus
3 Barcketh	Marble	Gemini
4 Nofek	Chrysoprase	Cancer
5 Shosham	Sardonyx	Leo
6 Jashpeh	Jasper	Virgo
7 Lesham	Opal	Libra
8 Shebo	Banded Agate	Scorpio
9 Achlamah	Amethyst	Sagittarius
10 Tharshish	Serpentine	Capricorn
11 Sapir	Lapis Lazuli	Aquarius
12 Jaholom	Crystal	Pisces

elements. It was said that the jewels were set in a ring of brass and iron, the metals of Venus and Mars, so that Solomon could summon good genies with the Venus part of the ring and command evil spirits with the Martian iron. The belief that good fortune came with the gift of a precious stone was, and still is, widespread:

As a precious stone appeareth a prize in the eyes of him that obtaineth it; withersoever it turneth it prospereth. *Proverbs* 17:8

According to the Talmud, Abraham wore a magical stone with the power to heal sickness. When the angelic Elohim blessed the nation, the gem in Aaron's ring was said to shine brilliantly. It was also believed that when the wearer and the gem were in harmony, the brightness reflected the conditions surrounding him. Pope Gregory the Great assigned gemstones to each of the ascending orders of angels, allocating emerald to the most high angel

princes. It was believed the gems would attract to their
wearer the associated, angelic order.

In the Buddhist tradition, there are seven royal
treasures and seven precious minerals, which are gold,
silver, pearls (or lapis lazuli in some sources), sapphires or
rubies (both are corundrum), cat's eyes, diamonds and
corals.

SUPERNATURAL POWERS

Probably the earliest crystal mines were in the Sinai
Peninsula. From about 3400 B.C., slaves mined turquoise
to adorn the pharaohs of Ancient Egypt. The world's
oldest surviving jewellery, bracelets belonging to Queen
Zer of Egypt, contain carved Sinai turquoise. Early
Egyptian lore said that the heavens were made of stone.
Hathor was the goddess of the turquoise stones and other
deities were represented in different carved gemstones.
Carnelian, turquoise, lapis lazuli and occasionally obsidian
were the stones most often used.

Lapis lazuli was so highly prized by the Egyptians
that they imported supplies from Afghanistan, 2,500 miles
away, to supplement their own production. These and
other stones were used extensively to make amulets and
charms, not only by the Egyptians but by the Babylonians
and Assyrians also. A seal made of rock crystal was
supposed to increase material possessions, one of lapis
lazuli to contain a god, while green serpentine was
believed to attract good luck. The beautiful blue lapis
lazuli crystal was associated by the Sumerians with the
dog star Sirius. They connected the heavenly bodies with
gemstones through their colour associations. So the red
and rosy stones were linked with Mars, green stones
belonged to Venus, blue was for Mercury, violet for

Saturn and light blues reflected the distant mountain
snows that came during the reign of Jupiter.

Colour still plays an important role in crystal healing,
as we know that different colours affect energy by
vibrating at different rates. Out of the ancient Indian
healing tradition, a system of vibrational therapy was
developed in the 1940s by Dr Benoytosh Bhattacharyya.
This system uses the colour vibrations of the gems to
treat various ailments by balancing the energy spectrum
in the individual.

THE BLACK STONE OF MECCA

Each of the major world religions has associations with
stones. In Islam, the most famous is the Black Stone of
Mecca. Originally said to be pure white, the stone became
black with the sins of humankind but is still believed to be
shining white at its heart. The legend states that when
Adam and Eve were turned out of the Garden of Eden,
a special stone fell to earth with them. After the great
flood this stone was returned to paradise but was then
given to Abraham by the angel Gabriel. Abraham set it
in the south eastern corner of the Ka'bah in Mecca.

The Black Stone was eventually taken from Mecca
by the Karmatians, a sect who had overturned the
fundamental points of Islam, and it took twenty-two years
for the stone to be returned. Today, the stone, 'the right
hand of god on earth', is most highly revered by pilgrims
to Mecca and is shaped from countless devoted touches.

FATED DIAMONDS

Since diamonds were first discovered, these hardest of all
crystals have inspired a wealth of lore. They were long ago
believed to make their wearer unconquerable and it is said

that the garden of delights, the fifth Arabian heaven, is composed of the purest diamonds. Diamonds were always a symbol of purity and a powerful charm against evil. They often carry dramatic histories, sometimes even involving the fortunes of kings, queens and nations. Stolen diamonds have brought dire misfortune to their owners, as some of the following stories — just a few from the many collected by Isadore Kosminsky — show.

The Koh-i-Noor diamond, now a part of the British Crown Jewels, was never lucky for India, where it had an evil reputation. When Nadir Shah of Persia conquered Delhi in 1739, he took the stone and named it Koh-i-Noor or 'mountain of light'. Nadir Shah was murdered for the stone on his journey home and the diamond passed via further misfortune to Runjeet Singh who, on his deathbed, sent it for safekeeping to the Temple of Juggernaut. When the British annexed the Punjab in 1849, it was presented to Queen Victoria by the East India Company. Indian ill-fortune continued and within ten years India was almost totally ruled by the British Crown. Water that had contained the Koh-i-Noor was believed to cure all diseases.

The Orloff Diamond, originally the eye stone in a statue of Brahma, was stolen from a temple in Mysore by a French soldier. It came via a London dealer into the possession of Prince Orloff, who presented it to the Empress Catherine the Great of Russia. Catherine had it mounted in the royal sceptre, which some believe influenced the subsequent ill-fortune of the Russian Royal Family.

The Hope Diamond, a strange blue stone, also brought terrible misfortune to its owners. It was acquired by Louis XIV for the French royal house and it carried the family fortunes finally to the guillotine. After the death of

Louis XVI and Marie Antoinette, it was stolen along with the rest of the Crown treasures. It changed hands several times, accompanied by more tales of theft, betrayal and death, until it passed to the Hope family in the nineteenth century. But their fortunes declined also and so it was sold to the Russian Prince Kanitovski, who went insane soon afterwards. The prince lent it to his lady love, who was wearing it when he suffered a fit and shot her. He himself was murdered in the street days later.

The horror continued when the diamond came into the hands of a Greek jeweller, who was killed with his wife and two children in a driving accident after selling the diamond to Sultan Abdul Hamid.

These stories illustrate the way that energies — for good and ill — can be held and even gather momentum as a stone is passed on. No doubt the reputation of such infamous jewels carries a huge power of itself, which has a great influence on the mind, but the legends begin with stones which are themselves revered power objects. The energies of the stone and the minds of those it influences reinforce each other.

A GLOBAL PATTERN OF BELIEF

Even in a brief look at the history of crystals, a near global pattern of belief emerges. Crystals and gemstones originally come from, or are at least connected with, heavenly spirits or gods, linking the spirit worlds with humanity. They have the power to effect healing cures, to enhance perception, to endow psychic powers and to bring power and protection or disaster to the bearer. Looked at from a different viewpoint, you could say that crystals help humans expand beyond their accustomed limits, to step outside their normal world.

CHAPTER THREE

Caring for Yourself and Your Crystals

As a healer you need to be as 'clear' as possible — a consideration that extends to handling crystals. Don't treat others when you are out of sorts, as you run the risk of stealing their energy. Instead, give yourself the healing space you need and invite the appropriate crystal to help you to restore your own energy balance.

CLEANLINESS

Physically you should maintain the highest possible standards of hygiene. Dirt attracts and holds negative energies such as fear, anger and pain. So do make sure that your body, hair and clothes are really clean. It is even a good idea to keep clothes especially for your healing work.

CHOOSING QUARTZ CRYSTALS

The flashiest is not necessarily the best, or most powerful. Consider the use you have in mind for the crystal. Do you want clear quartz or rose or amethyst? Do you want a focusing and personal crystal (a single point) or a cluster, for more general influences?

Quartz crystals come in many shapes and sizes, but all share the characteristics of having six sides, or faces, and two ends. Single terminated quartz crystals have one pointed end — or termination — the crystal having grown from a bed in the earth. The energetic flow of the crystal is outwards from the termination. Double terminated quartz crystals have a termination point at both ends, having grown freely in opposite directions.

They are less common and are powerful balancers when used in healing. Some stones are called massive — that is, they are not visibly crystalline and have an irregular form. These stones are most often sold commercially as tumblestones or cut and polished for jewellery, although uncut specimens are available from specialist crystal suppliers and may have stronger energetic properties.

Perfect points and clusters are expensive. Slightly damaged crystals are fine for home and office use and especially for 'heavy work' such as screening electrical radiation (see Chapter Four). There are books that go into intricate detail about the exact form of individual crystals — the number or sides on the faces, triangles, diamonds and so on. But this is specialist information — to begin with I think it is better to choose with your heart and not your head. Centre yourself, slow your breathing and scan the crystals until you find one that especially draws or calls to you. You will know it when you find it. Spend a few moments examining the crystal in the light. Enjoy and marvel at the beautiful facets, rainbows, galaxies, etc. Then close your eyes and form a link with your crystal.

SPHERES, PYRAMIDS AND POLISHED STONES

If you wish to work with specially cut crystals, you should bear in mind that any imposed changes to the crystal's natural form will affect the way it works. Tumblestones are usually made from chips of damaged crystal or from crystals that are massive in structure, such as rose quartz. They are widely available and very useful in crystal healing. Tumbling tends to soften and decrease the effect of the stone, which for beginners is no bad thing.

Spheres are very popular, because the form reflects an all-round, all-encompassing radiance. This is usually beneficial, but the crystal's direction of growth and structure will also remain held within the created form. If you attempt a meditation (see Chapter Five, page 42) to enter a crystal sphere, you may find the lack of 'gravity' disorientating, but it is good way to experience the type of energy you are working with. Any geometry deliberately superimposed on a crystal will give a particular focus, but it is essential that the crystal be cut sympathetically. The gem cutter knows that incorrect cutting can kill the fire and irreparably damage a valuable stone.

A well-cut pyramid might be a good choice for the central focus of a meditation room or group, the structure holding a particularly balanced geometry that will influence the mind and the energy field in the room. A crystal wand that has been knowledgeably polished along the crystal's natural geometry can greatly strengthen the effect of the crystal. However, in this book I will concentrate on the use of unpolished and tumbled stones.

TAKING CARE OF CRYSTALS

Crystals like the sun, fresh spring and sea water — keep them on a sunny shelf or window-sill and as dust free as possible.

GENERAL CLEANSING

For quartz:

2 tablespoonfuls sea salt

to 2 pts spring water

Soak the crystal/s in the solution for at least one hour (up to 6 hours if the crystal is very tired or comes from a

shop where its history is unknown). Rinse in clear
spring water and pat dry with a soft white cotton cloth.
Then place for at least 4 hours in sunlight, preferably
outside. Full moonlight is also good and using both sun-
and moonlight will balance the masculine and feminine
energies.

Cleansing should be done as often as needed —
for crystals used in the home at least once a fortnight,
or sooner if they look dull and depleted. Healing crystals
should be quick-cleansed after each session by running
them under a cold tap point downwards for a few
moments, or by using the breath as described below.
Meditation crystals kept exclusively for your own use
will not need such frequent cleansing, as your own
energy will tend to blend with the crystal's energy and
keep you both well. If you use a crystal for frequent
energy boosts, however, make sure it gets recharged in
sunlight and/or salt water regularly.

Rainwater is a gentle medium for cleansing crystals.
It should be collected in a clear glass or natural container
(a wooden barrel is ideal). You can then bathe the
crystals in the usual way, omitting the salt. Sea water
is another cleansing medium and your crystals will
love the sea energy that it brings. Sacred well or spring
water will bring the special blessing of the site from
which the water comes — a marvellous treatment for
healing crystals.

STONES NEEDING SPECIAL CLEANSING
Some crystals cannot be cleansed in the usual way. A
friend of mine supplied halite crystals to a healer, who
later reported a remarkable thing had happened — she
left them to clean in water overnight and they completely

vanished! This was not the miracle she supposed, however — halite is water soluble.

Listed below are stones with special needs.

Stones that disintegrate or are damaged in water

Apophyllite

Azurite

Bornite

Calcites

Celestite

Citrine (very often artificially heat-treated
Amethyst, may be fragile)

Gypsums

Halites (salts)

Selenite

Talc

Stones that hate detergents

Azurite

Chrysocolla

Fluorite

Malachite

ALTERNATIVE CLEANSING METHODS

When stones are not treated gently and respectfully, the results can be most unfortunate. You should cleanse and store stones of varying hardness separately, as soft stones will be damaged by contact with harder ones. Crystals such as celestite, calcite and apophyllite crumble very easily. So what do you do? There are many ways of cleansing crystals and I have listed my favourites below. Clear intention and sincerity make all the difference in cleansing rites.

Smudging

This is the Native American way to purify, which
involves burning a combination of desert sage, sweet grass
and cedar. You can obtain these herbs in some health
stores and New Age shops in the form of a smudge stick
(a bound bundle of these herbs), or loose. I suggest you do
this outdoors or somewhere safe, away from precious rugs
or furniture, in case of flying sparks.

You need:

a large shell (abalone is traditional) *or* heatproof bowl

a fan *or* bundle of feathers

matches

Place the loose herbs or smudge stick in the shell
or bowl and light them until they begin to burn. When
the surface is burning well, use the fan to extinguish
the flame, leaving the herbs smouldering and smoking.
First, smudge yourself by drawing the smoke with
cupped hand to your heart centre, over your head,
down your arms and down the front and back of your
body to the ground.

Traditionally, you then offer the smoke to the six
directions; upwards to spirit, down to mother earth,
then to the north, east, south and west. Although this is
the order of the Native American tradition, you may be
more familiar with starting in the east through south,
west and north then below and finishing above. Use
the sequence you are most comfortable with, but move
clockwise in the direction of the sun. After the offering,
you can smudge each of your crystals individually,
consecrating them with sacred smoke. You can also
smudge the room you are working in, paying special
attention to the corners, doors and windows. Incense
can be used in a similar way.

Quick individual crystal cleansing

One of the most effective ways of cleansing, this method needs no props whatsoever. It is a very effective technique, taken from the excellent *The Newcastle Guide to Healing with Crystals* by Pamela Chase and Jonathan Pawlik, for cleansing and charging your crystals.

For quartz points, hold the crystal, point upwards, with your index finger on the largest pyramidal facet and inhale deeply. Hold your breath briefly, while you visualise and affirm any imbalance of energy being transformed and the crystal clearing. Continue this visualisation while you exhale slowly through your nostrils on to the crystal. Do this several times until the crystal feels as if it's been cleared. If you feel it's necessary, you can also visualise a fountain of light flowing from the base to the point, and flowing all round the crystal and working from the centre out to the sides. You can use this method for tumblestones equally effectively.

DEEP HEALING

Sometimes you find crystals that need deep healing. The best thing is to bury the crystal in the soil and let it receive the comfort of mother earth. A rose quartz came to me once that was quite grey and so drained it literally looked sick. I buried it in a flowerbed near the front door, leaving a little piece showing so I could find it again. I left it there, turning and checking it occasionally, for about six months. When finally I took it up, it was a bright warm pink and radiated the gentle energy that is its natural healthy state. If you bury small stones, mark the spot well, or bury them in a clay pot with the rim left showing. In exceptional cases you may find it necessary to leave a stone in the ground indefinitely.

CHARGING INDIVIDUAL CRYSTALS

It is important to dedicate your working crystals and, as in all areas of your practice, intention is vital. A general thought intention that the crystal works 'with love and light for the highest good of all whom it contacts' is a good all-round dedication. But you could ask for special help in healing, use a prayer of dedication or blessing, or visualise a symbol of balance and unity such as the cross within the circle, the sun or a radiant six-pointed star. Once again using the breath and holding the crystal as described above, inhale, hold your breath and visualise the crystal being charged with light, vitality and love. Remember, energy follows thought. Continue while you exhale in short bursts through your nose on to the crystal. Repeat several times until you are satisfied that the job is done.

The shamanic traditions emphasise the part of the elements in charging crystals. There is no doubt that crystals are empowered by being placed on the earth (some traditions suggest in a high place) to be charged by the light of the sun and the moon, especially at powerful times — when the moon is full or new and at the summer or winter solstice.

STORING

When travelling, wrap your crystals in soft, white, natural fibre such as silk, linen or cotton. Shamans carry their crystals in hide medicine bags or in little thonged leather pouches around their necks. At home, let crystals live on sunny shelves and window-sills if possible. Personal crystals should not be passed around or displayed publicly if you want them to hold their charge.

CHAPTER FOUR

Sacred Space

There is mounting evidence to suggest that electrical radiation may contribute to a variety of illnesses. The sources of this radiation include overhead power cables, domestic appliances and power sockets. Another source of illness is 'geopathic stress' a natural radiation usually generated by underground watercourses. The energy is carried up through the house and is most troublesome in areas directly over the geopathic 'wave'. Those who are already ill or run-down are most likely to be sensitive to its harmful effects. It can also enter electrical cables, sub-stations and pylons, reaching our homes and workplaces through electrical appliances such as storage heaters, computers, microwave ovens and electric blankets.

While researching the causes of his wife's illness, Dr Mike Adams came to disturbing conclusions about the effects of radiation from ordinary 13 amp sockets. Power socket radiation can apparently only be picked up directly through the top of the head, but can also invade our food and drink. Dr Adams suggests the combined effects of direct and 'consumed' radiation may be responsible for fatigue, insomnia and illnesses such as multiple sclerosis, ME and cancers. Blocking off the source of the radiation leakage is a sensible preventative measure and may contribute to recovery where illness already exists. Dr Adams found that this could be tackled using quartz crystals.

All single and double terminated clear quartz crystals and crystals from the quartz group (rose, amethyst, citrine, etc.) will work to return radiation into the sockets and even to prevent it entering the house cables altogether.

A large crystal (7–10 cm/3–5 in long and about 4 cm/
1¾ in across) or cluster can be placed to the side of the
main fuse box, with the main point or points facing away,
or on top of the fuse box laid lengthways parallel to the
wall. A small natural crystal point worn as a pendant will
give permanent protection if cleansed daily. Large fuse
box crystals should be cleansed thoroughly once a month.
I have two crystals for this heavy-duty work, so they work
one month on and take one month's holiday!

It is possible to test for electrical radiation leakages
using an ordinary hand-held compass. Align your compass
so that the arrow faces north and approach the appliance
steadily. If there is any disturbance in the electromagnetic
field, the compass needle will fluctuate. When testing this
technique a few years ago, I discovered to my horror that
our electric blanket made the compass needle oscillate
wildly, even though the blanket was switched off at the
time. A quartz cluster placed under the bed sorted out the
blanket and I keep a crystal cluster in front of my computer
screen. Appliances to check are those that get frequent use
such as microwave ovens, TVs and computers.

Dr Adams makes the point that we have all adapted
to receiving these power socket waves and so may expect
to suffer a worsening of symptoms or 'withdrawal' during
the first week following setting up the crystal protections.
Bach Flowers Rescue Remedy will help.

Geopathic stress is very often tackled by dowsing the
house to determine the direction and flow of stress, then
burying copper rods (copper piping, cut to the length of
the dowsed stress wave) in the ground outside to interrupt
the flow at the point of entry. While effective, this method
is not always practicable. An easier approach is to create a
crystal grid. Crystal grids set up a pristine, balanced energy

field and can be used to create sacred space for healing and meditation. The basic principle involves a geometric pattern of crystals which creates a contained and clear space.

About two years ago, I was staying with a dear friend, Gabrielle. It was a wet winter's evening and she complained that her bedroom was always cold despite the central heating. She often woke with bad dreams and had difficulty getting back to sleep. It sounded like a case of geopathic stress, but it was dark and wet and the prospect of dowsing and digging did not appeal, so we set up a crystal grid instead. Using four medium-sized quartz points, we placed one in each corner of the room, pointed end towards the centre (so, if you joined up the points with imaginary lines, you would create a large X with the lines bisecting at the centre).

Gabrielle slept well that night, but a few days later I had a call from her to say an odd thing had happened. She woke in the night and noticed a faint light in the corner of the room. As it is an old house, she assumed she must have left a light on downstairs that was shining through the floorboards. But she found no lights on. The crystal we had placed in that corner was actually glowing — the geopathic energy that had been causing the disturbance was being interrupted and converted into light.

CRYSTAL HEALING GRIDS AND THE POWER OF NUMBERS

The cross-quarter room grid can be used not only against geopathic stress but also in setting up a sacred space. As it is easily transported, it can be used to 'clear' a hotel room, make a temporary healing space or to keep the home and work space balanced and harmonious. The same principle of geometric grids can be applied outdoors at the corners of the house or garden.

Because of the vibration and proportion inherent in
different numbers, a grid of four will have a different effect
to that of six, and so on. Placing a person's photograph
or a treasured personal object within a sacred crystal grid
can positively affect the owner. Try the six-pointed Star
of David grid and see if you notice a difference. An
astrologer might be interested in the effects of setting up
a grid on the birthchart to offset difficult aspects. This is
'magical' thinking of a high order, but I have seen
instances where it has been very effective. Experiment
and record your results.

ONE

The number of the pioneering individual, independence
and potential individuation. Not strictly a grid, but a
centre of power. One crystal will radiate energy and have a
spreading effect. To use with a group of people in a circle,
place a large single crystal at the centre to unify the energy
of the group, or as a central focus for group meditation.

TWO

The number of relationship and polarity, two balances
polarities — top and bottom, front and back, opposite
sides, male and female, inner and outer, yin and yang —
it bounces and equalises energy. You can use two crystals
in all sorts of ways, including the following.

Energy clearing and boosting

Hold a clear quartz point in each hand, one facing away
and one facing into the body according to the way you
are polarised (see Chapter Four, page 00 for information
on how to determine your polarity). Variations include two
crystals likewise at the feet. This balances your own energy.

Personal sacred space

Place a quartz point (point towards you) or cluster on the floor at the front and back of your chair or at the top and bottom of your bed. This creates a harmonious space for relaxation and healing.

Polar balance

Again, using a compass, determine true north and place one crystal in the north and the other in the south to align the room's energies with the poles of the earth.

THREE

The power of three is associated with creative self-expression and the joy of living. The Trinity symbolises the union of spirit, energy and matter, which creates manifestation. This is dynamic, energetic life! Matthew Goodwin says that it is through the number three that the artist finds expression — writing, painting, sculpting, singing, composing — and it is through three that we express our feelings for others. This number has a lovely energy of enthusiasm and optimism. A grid of three is excellent for the artist's studio or writer's study.

Creative trines

Place the crystals at the base of the triangle pointing toward the apex of the triangle, with the crystal at the apex of the triangle (1) its point inwards to bring creative inspiration; or (2) its point outwards, to assist creative expression. The exact placing of the creative trine grid will depend on the form of creativity. For example, in a studio the grid may be placed so that the apex is near the artist wishing to be inspired or near the canvas, which is the point of expression.

FOUR

Four is the square, the symbol for earth. Its energy is, as you might expect, grounded, containing, well ordered and well earthed. Particularly useful for earth related matters or when there is the need to have your feet on the ground (a good idea in most healing situations). It is also associated with limitation in the service of others.

Cross-quarter

This grid, described on page 29, is well balanced and good for earthing energy.

The four directions

Use this variation to balance the elemental influences according to the four directions of the compass. Discover the exact compass alignments of the room or space you wish to influence and place a crystal at east, south, west and north, pointed tip facing centre as above.

FIVE

The pentagram star, associated with the five elements of earth, water, fire, air and ether or spirit. The balancing of these five elements is central to western esoteric thought and occurs in many other traditions, notably ayurveda. The lesson of five is not to dissipate energy and potential, but to balance the elements to bring about expansion and limitless potential.

Sacred five

The finest use of five for an environmental grid is to place spirit at the centre of a square grid of four. In other words, place your crystals as suggested above in the cross-quartered or four directions layout and place a fifth crystal at the centre of the grid to symbolise the energy of spirit.

If it is possible to hang the crystal, point downwards, at the centre of a room, you will feel the balance of four and the sacred potential of five. If you cannot hang the crystal, place a crystal, point upwards, on the floor or on a table at the centre. The energy is slightly different in each case.

The pentagram ray

This is for a group. Place the quartz points in the centre of the room, on the floor or on a table, points outwards in the five-pointed star formation.

Six

The six-pointed star, the Star of David, is a double triangle associated with the balancing impulses of spirit invested in matter and matter in spirit. One triangle points upwards, reaching to spirit from an earthed base; the other triangle pushes down from spirit and pierces matter. It is also the synthesis of the masculine and feminine principles — the union of these energies is beautifully realised in the six-pointed star. This is one of the finest energies to work with for healing and spiritual work.

The Star of David

For a chair grid, take six cleansed single terminated quartz points. Place each one on the floor about 50 cm/20 in from the body, pointing inwards, one behind at centre, one in front between the feet, one aligned with each shoulder and one aligned with each knee.

For a lying down grid, place each quartz point about 50 cm/20 in from the body, pointing inwards, one above the head, one beneath the feet, one level with each shoulder and one level with each knee. This elongates the star, but is equally effective (see Illustration 1).

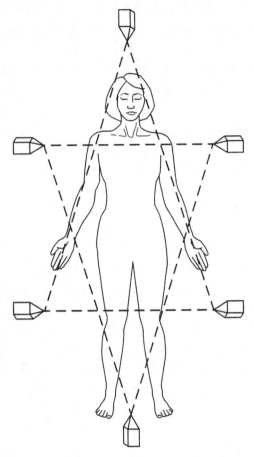

Illustration 1: Star of David Grid

The Star of David ray

This one is great for a meditation group. Place the quartz points in the centre of the room, on the floor or on a table, points outwards in the star formation, to create a beautiful atmosphere of harmony and peace.

SEVEN

Seven is an introspective number and grids of seven are good for self-analysis, self-knowledge and all inner work.

Concerned with spiritual rather than material realities and values, seven encourages deep study and meditation.

The seven-rayed star
This grid, which sets seven crystals, points inward, evenly around the sacred space, brings an energy of high mental attunement and encourages understanding and insight.

EIGHT
Eight, as double four, has a lot to teach us about material reality and the lessons of functioning in, and understanding the energy of, the material world. However, tackling personal limitations is vital if real mastery is to be accomplished. Eight requires awareness of limitations and has rather a heavy energetic quality.

Double square
The grid to bring you right up against self-limitation and restriction. Useful occasionally when working with these energies, it may bring greater understanding. Place the crystals point inwards at each corner and then halfway between each corner, creating a second square. It may feel quite claustrophobic.

NINE
Nine is a magical number, the flipside of one. It is about the power of giving away power. St Francis said, 'it is in giving that we receive'. Service to humanity is paramount in the individual working with nine, either directly serving others or in giving through creative expression.

Nine is associated with the deep mysteries of the self in relation to the all, microcosm and macrocosm. Energy spirals inwards to the centre then returns out toward the whole in a constant dance or double helix. This spiralling energy is more 'feminine' and intuitive than 'masculine' and constructive. The nine sisters at the cauldron of Cerridwen, the nine Muses and, in Arthurian legend, the nine sisters of Avalon, give us a sense of the archetypal significance and mysterious power spun by the nine.

Spiral of nine

The best grid for nine is a spiral form. To use this grid for meditation, start by marking out the spiral on the ground (follow the illustration) with a ball of string, cord or roll of tape. Without this guide you will get in a muddle. The diameter for the complete spiral should be as large as space allows, but approximately 2.5–3 metres for an indoor spiral and, ideally, at least 4 metres outdoors.

Next, using nine crystals, start with crystal one at the centre; moving outwards and clockwise, place 2 in the north east; continue clockwise to place 3 in the south east; 4 in the south west; and continuing outwards, 5 in the north west. Move out and round to place 6 in the east, 7 in the west, 8 in the north and lastly 9 in the south.

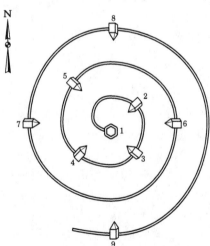

Illustration 2: Spiral of Nine

For a very strong focus to the centre, using quartz points, place the crystals facing anti-clockwise along the path of the spiral towards the centre. For a dispersing energy, place the crystal points clockwise. Or place them turned all to the centre or all rayed outwards. Experiment and see which suits you best. It will very much depend on your purpose. A gentler and very lovely grid can be made using lumps of rough rose quartz. Another variation is to use clusters or a cluster at the centre, or a combination of any of these.

Working with the spiral of nine will open you up to the mysteries, the nature of life and reality. This layout is magnificent placed outdoors, or at least where there is enough space for you to walk the spiral as a moving meditation, meditating at the centre, then returning out through the spiral, transformed. In Chapter Seven you will find a meditation to use with this spiral grid.

There are of course many more numbers, geometries and possible grids, but the information in this chapter should give you a foundation on which to build. In a typical layout for a healing room, I use a cross-quarter or a sacred five grid for the room as a whole and then set up the appropriate personal energy grid for my client, often a Star of David. Within this other crystals may also be placed, depending on the type of treatment being given.

FENG SHUI

The Chinese art of geomancy, feng shui (pronounced 'foong shway') is very practical and can effectively transform your life, along with your environment and the sort of energy it attracts. Prosperity, harmony and peace can be created where formerly there was depression and lack. It offers us a way of moving back into harmony with, and a cooperative understanding of, our environment. You will find some excellent books on the market describing its principles, but one I specially treasure is William Spear's *Feng Shui Made Easy*.

Crystals can be used to activate *chi* energy in feng shui. According to their properties, they will affect the vibrational environment you live in. It is essential that they are kept clean. The crystal you wear is an active centre of *chi* and it will energise or deplete your energy depending on it's condition. A bright amethyst cluster could be a boon in the study, as it will help to align you with higher mental vibrations; whereas a chunk of rose quartz can bring a sense of affection and well-being to the bedroom, encouraging restful sleep and sweet dreams.

Glass 'crystals' hung in the light are wonderful for spreading the moving rainbow colours of the light spectrum through the room. The best choice is one of symmetrical shape (sphere, oval, tear-drop, etc.) and of medium size (about 25 cm/10 in diameter) — too large or irregular and they unbalance the energy in the room. These artificial crystals do not have the same vibrational properties as the crystals described in this book, but they do create waves of light which are valuable in themselves. The placement of a crystal, natural or artificial, in a dark corner will reflect light, add positive energy and move *chi* where there might otherwise be stagnation.

Crystals can be used effectively alone or with other feng shui cures, but mirrors and windchimes should be removed from the immediate environment of the crystal, as the mix can cause imbalances — a case of less is more. A crystal placed in the *tai chi*, that is at the uniting centre of the space, changes the energy of the whole environment and can provide a very powerful cure.

CHAPTER FIVE

The Sacred Self

As well as the vast sea of energy which I call life force, there is an individual energy field called the aura, surrounding the human body. It takes the shape of a gigantic egg.

During the 1930s, Dr Harold Saxton Burr, Anatomy Professor at Yale, became interested in the electrical potential of living things. He set up measuring equipment which successfully detected electrical field phenomena associated with trees and other plants, many animals — including humans — and even slime moulds. Such fields are not static. A voltmeter attached to a tree will, for example, indicate fluctuations in response to light, moisture, storms, sunspots and moon phase.

Burr came to believe in the existence of a life-field, which, in the words of Dr Lyall Watson, 'holds the shape of an organism just as a mould determines the shape of a pie or pudding'. Dr Burr's theories were largely ignored by the scientific establishment throughout much of his working life, even though they went a long way towards explaining one of the most persistent mysteries of cellular biology. Simply stated, the mystery is how certain cells in your body 'knew' how to grow into a kidney, while others grew into a brain.

It is evident that some sort of organising principle is involved in living matter, and scientists have devoted substantial effort in a vain attempt to isolate chemical or other triggers of the process. Dr Burr's life-field certainly seems to fit the bill. While orthodox science still seems reluctant to discuss the theory, practical experience has very clearly established an electrical aspect to the human body. Technology has advanced so far since the time Burr first tried to measure a life-field that an investment of less than £100 will buy you equipment sufficiently sensitive to detect fluctuations in the electrical potential of the skin.

This idea runs very close to very old concepts about a second body. There seems very little difference between Burr's life-field and the esoteric notion of a subtle body, except, perhaps, in one important respect. Dr Burr suggests that the field is an integral part of a living creature, a phenomenon of living matter, possibly even the factor which, ultimately, differentiates between the animate and the inanimate. It is the esoteric belief, by contrast, that the life-field may be temporarily separated from the physical body and become the vehicle of consciousness and perception. This is the process of so-called 'astral projection'.

KIRLIAN PHOTOGRAPHY

The idea of an energy system associated with the human body goes further. Kirlian photography involves a specially constructed high frequency oscillator. The object to be investigated is inserted between the clamps, along with photographic paper. The generator is switched on and a high frequency field is created between the clamps, which apparently causes the object to radiate some sort of bio-luminescence on to the paper.

Kirlian pictures which involved living tissue — even plant tissue like a leaf — show sparks and flares of energy in patterns as dramatic as they are beautiful. A dead leaf shows nothing of these patterns. When a portion of a leaf is torn or cut away, a ghostly image of the missing piece remains. Kirlian photographs of human volunteers confirm that the aura effect varies in relation to mood and personality interactions: the Kirlian auras of young men brighten when a pretty woman enters the room.

Extensive investigation of Kirlian photography, electromagnetic fields, the idea of morphogenic fields (as developed by Rupert Sheldrake) and the concept that there is a pattern of wholeness in the living organism even if part of the physical whole is removed (a 'holographic' life pattern), has led UK-based Harry Oldfield to develop a whole system of electrocrystal therapy. The trained practitioner uses a device that utilises an applied electrical field, amplified by quartz crystals, to realign imbalanced energy and promote healing. Oldfield's results are as impressive as his ongoing research. He sees health intrinsically linked with energy balancing and that we are made of nothing but patterns of resonant energy.

THE WAY YOUR ENERGY FLOWS

For effective energy healing, it is very helpful to know how you, or the person you are working with, is 'polarised'. We all have a receiving side and a giving side, with which we take in energy and send it out. This is most often applied to the hands, but also applies to the body as a whole, as you will see in some of the crystal layouts that follow.

Our giving hand (or + charge) is very often the same as the hand we write with; our other hand (or - charge) is more receptive and sensitive — an important faculty for the healer for tuning into and picking up impressions from the patient. It is not invariably the case, however, as our polarity can switch at times of life changes, extreme stress or trauma. One good way of checking your polarity is with a quartz point.

First, rub your hands together briskly. Now take a
natural quartz crystal in your left hand, point outwards,
then gently 'comb' your right palm from your wrist
towards your fingertips, keeping the point about 5 mm/⅙ in
from the surface of the skin. Remember that this is subtle
work, so allow yourself to be relaxed and quietly receptive
and don't rush it. You will start to experience some small
physical sensation — a breeze, heat, cold, prickling, as the
crystal passes above the surface of your palm.

When you have a reaction, swap the crystal over to
your right hand and repeat the process over your left palm.
Whichever hand feels the sensation of the crystal energy
most strongly is your receiving (or - charge) hand (and
side). The less sensitive is your giving (or + charge) hand.
This information gives you something that can be applied
to many of the crystal healing techniques and layouts
described in this book and which will stand you in good
stead for any healing and sensitive work you undertake.

Connecting with your Crystal
When you have chosen a natural quartz crystal point for
yourself that you want to get to know and work with, I
suggest you follow the following simple procedure.

Personal Attunement to the Light
It is always good practice to begin your meditation or
crystal work by attuning yourself to the light or to your
own sense of the source of highest good.

Crystal Cleansing
Make sure your crystal is cleansed. If you have not done so
already, do it now. (Several methods are given in Chapter
Three.) The breath method, as follows, is quick and

effective: hold the crystal, point upwards, with your index finger on the largest pyramidal facet and inhale deeply. Hold your breath briefly while you visualise and affirm any imbalance of energy being transformed and the crystal clearing. Continue this visualisation while you exhale slowly through your nostrils on to the crystal. Do this several times until the crystal feels as if it's been cleared.

CHARGING YOUR CRYSTAL

The next step is to charge your crystal. Once again using the breath and holding the crystal as described above, inhale, hold your breath and visualise the crystal being charged with light, vitality and love. Continue while you exhale in short bursts through your nose on to the crystal. Repeat several times until you are satisfied that the job is done. Complete the preparation with an affirmation that the crystal may be filled with love and life-force energy.

EXPLORING YOUR CRYSTAL

Your chosen crystal is as unique as you are, so spend a few minutes examining it in the light. Enjoy the surface texture, feel the smoothness or the naturally 'etched' markings on your crystal — sometimes you will find regular triangles or what appear to be like hieroglyphs with encoded messages! Now look within the crystal and marvel at the beautiful facets, rainbows, galaxies, whole worlds inside it. Then close your eyes and remember as much as you can about your crystal, opening them again to check your memories. Alternate this, eyes open, eyes closed, a few times until you feel that you know the appearance of your crystal.

I recommend that you follow this visual exploration of your crystal with a meditation that takes you inside the crystal (see Entering the Crystal, Chapter Seven, pages 63–66). Do this meditation with any quartz crystal you want to work with — it will connect you with the crystal more deeply than any other method I know.

BALANCING THE AURA WITH CRYSTALS

Crystals are very effective in correcting imbalance or damage in the aura. There are several useful and simple methods you can safely use at home, applying first the basic principles of healing which is (1) clear or cleanse; then (2) re-energise or boost. Creating and holding a sacred space has been discussed in the previous chapter — now you can move on to ways of clearing, re-balancing and energising the aura. Always make sure you have cleansed and charged all your crystals before you start work.

As a general rule, quartz points used with the point directed away from the body will clear and draw off excess or imbalance in the energy field. Quartz points directed towards the body tend to introduce energy or contain an energy field.

AURA CLEARING

The simplest method for clearing with a quartz point is to hold the crystal in the palm of your giving hand (see The Way your Energy Flows, above) with the point outwards towards your middle fingertip. A few minutes is all it takes, especially if you assist the work by using your breath and visualisation. Breathe in slowly and deeply, allowing your belly to extend and your chest and shoulders to be soft and relaxed, visualising pure clean air/light/life force filling you. On your out-breath, visualise letting go of all the disharmony, fear, upset, grunge and grime that you might be holding. Repeat until you feel free and clear. Move on straight away to the Energy Booster.

ENERGY BOOSTER

To boost your energy, simply swap hands, placing the
quartz point in your receiving hand, point towards your
wrist. Use your breath and visualise as with the Aura
Clearing, but this time imagine on your out-breath that
you are sending the air/light/life force to every cell and
atom of your body, boosting and protecting your whole
energy field. Repeat for several breaths or until you feel
calm and energised. Don't overdo the deep breathing,
as it can make you rather light-headed.

ENERGY CIRCUIT

Using two quartz points, you can combine the two
methods described above in clearing and energy boosting
at the same time. Take one quartz point in your giving
hand, point outwards, the other in your receiving hand,
point inward. This produces a very balanced energy
circuit which will be a quick pick-me-up at the end of
the day or whenever you need to re-balance yourself.

STAR OF DAVID

This is the same grid described in Chapter Four. It gives
a wonderfully harmonious and refreshing energy. Ten to
fifteen minutes in this grid will leave you feeling like
you've had a few hours sleep. For a chair grid, take six
cleansed, single terminated quartz points. Place each one
on the floor about 50 cm/20 in from the body, pointing
inwards, one behind at centre, one in front between the
feet, one aligned with each shoulder and one aligned
with each knee.

For a lying down grid (strongly recommended if
possible): place each quartz point about 50 cm/20 in
from the body, pointing inwards, one above the head,

one beneath the feet, one level with each shoulder and one level with each knee. This elongates the star but is equally effective (see Illustration 1 on page 34).

CLEANSING CLUSTERS

Clusters send energy in all directions and both amethyst and clear quartz clusters can be helpful in balancing, protecting and energising the aura. If you are lying down, using two clusters, place one a few inches above the crown of the head and another below the feet (or one cluster behind and in front of the chair, if you are sitting). One cluster underneath your chair can also be very effective.

Some of the other grids suggested in Chapter Four are suitable for personal aura work and it is interesting to note their different effects. Please bear in mind, though, that when you use crystal layouts to influence the aura, rather than the wider environment, special care is needed and the aim is always to balance. An over-complex layout is usually both unnecessary and undesirable.

MOVING ENERGY

An understanding of the meridian system of the body is very useful in crystal healing, although it is too complex a subject for the range of this book. A training in acupuncture is a long and serious commitment, but even a practical introductory course to shiatsu (Japanese finger pressure massage) is a good way to gain a basic grasp of the most detailed map of *chi* — or life force — flowing through our physical bodies. Crystals can be used with this system to help keep this vital energy network balanced and flowing. And some eastern medicine practitioners use quartz points to treat the *tsubos,* or energy points, on the meridians with great effect.

CHAPTER SIX

Crystals and the Chakras

The points of contact between universal and personal energy are known as the chakras — the connective channels of Oriental yoga and western esoteric practice. Chakra means wheel or vortex, an invisible centre of spinning energy, which is a focal point for receiving and transmitting energy at physical/social, sexual, emotional, mental and spiritual levels. The chakras act as a multi-levelled interface. Healers believe that by balancing and refining the energy flow through the chakras we can attain optimum health and well-being.

The most extensive work on chakras has been done in India, China and Tibet and has produced differing theories in all three cultures. This does not appear to influence results achieved by chakra manipulation and may actually be no more than a question of emphasis and perception (the power of belief influencing energy). It can, however, be confusing to a newcomer to chakra theory who needs a definitive location for each centre.

A study of Chinese acupuncture, which provides by far the most detailed chart of the human energy system, shows a multiplicity of control points — just under 400 according to traditional doctrine, with more being added each year with further investigation. This suggests that the chakras may be seen as *groupings* of control points, rather than a single energy centre. (Certainly there are lots of acupuncture points in each area associated with a chakra.) If this is so, then the association of a given chakra with specific points may be flexible. One system may hold that a group of points is associated with one chakra, while another system might subdivide the point grouping into two chakras. Either is equally viable.

The chakras act as transformers for the life force, enabling us to utilise it. Working with the chakras soon confirms that specific emotions, mental functions and states of consciousness are associated with individual chakras: intelligence and consciousness with the crown chakra, energy and sexuality with the base chakra, visionary experience with the brow chakra, communications problems with the throat, and so on.

The most common chakra system uses seven major chakras. It is especially convenient to use this system as a basis for crystal and gemstone healing, as the chakras can thus be symbolically linked to the seven colours of the light spectrum. This provides a balancing focus for meditation and self-healing, as I will describe.

Healers and mystics associate light with the life force, and crystals (especially clear quartz) have a special affinity with light because they transmit a broad range of the light spectrum — so much so, in fact, that they are often perceived as 'solid light'. Crystals are very effective in chakra balancing and certain stones have associations with particular chakras through their colour and energies.

THE CHAKRAS
Some of the associations with each of the chakras are given below. Remember that this is an interpenetrating, multi-dimensional system, so the information is only a guide:

1 BASE (MULADHARA CHAKRA) RED
Centred on base of the spine/pubic bone (or, according to some systems, the perineum between genitals and anus). The base chakra is associated with the earth, your

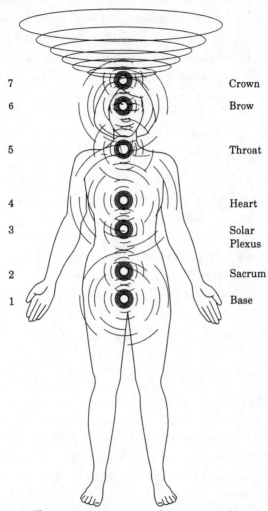

7   Crown

6   Brow

5   Throat

4   Heart

3   Solar Plexus

2   Sacrum

1   Base

Illustration 3: Location of 7 Major Chakras

foundation, the instinctual nature, the material world, social and material concerns and well-being. Adrenal gland, spinal column, kidneys. *Stones:* Red and black stones mostly — obsidian, hematite, smoky quartz, garnet, ruby, jasper, moss agate, carnelian, bloodstone.

2 SACRUM(SVADHISTHANA CHAKRA) ORANGE

Centred on the body's midline, four finger-widths below the navel. The sacral chakra is associated with sexuality, nourishment and emotion. This centre is divided in some systems: sex and emotion. Gonads, reproductive system. *Stones:* Carnelian, tiger's eye, rhodochrosite, bloodstone.

3 SOLAR PLEXUS (MANIPURA CHAKRA) YELLOW

Centred on the solar plexus. Associated with personal power, will, self-confidence, action. Pancreas, stomach, liver, gall-bladder, nervous system. *Stones:* Topaz, citrine, tiger's eye, sunstone, yellow calcite.

4 HEART (ANAHATA CHAKRA) GREEN

Centred on the midline at a level with the heart. Associated with unconditional love, self-acceptance, the movement for the purely personal to wider care and concern for others, free from attachments or expectations. Thymus, heart, blood, circulation. *Stones:* Green jade, malachite, aventurine, watermelon tourmaline, rose quartz, amazonite, peridot.

5 THROAT (VISUDDHA CHAKRA) SKY BLUE

Centred on the throat and extending to take in the lower part of the face. Associated with self-expression, communication of all kinds, creativity. Thyroid, bronchials, lungs, alimentary canal. *Stones:* Blue lace agate, lapis, blue chalcedony, turquoise, celestite, fluorite, aquamarine, moonstone.

6 BROW (AJNA CHAKRA) INDIGO

Centred between the eyebrows. Associated with mental thought, intuition and psychic development. Pituitary, lower brain, left eye, ears, nose, nervous system. *Stones:* Azurite, lapis lazuli, dumortiorite, sodalite, fluorite, sugilite, hawk's eye, celestite, clear quartz.

7 CROWN (SAHASRARA-PADMA CHAKRA) VIOLET-WHITE

Centred on the crown of the head. Associated with spirituality, connection with the godhead, the life force, the universal and cosmic energies. Pineal, upper brain, right eye. *Stones:* Clear quartz, amethyst, sugilite.

CRYSTAL LAYOUTS FOR THE CHAKRAS

Follow this simple layout for the chakras: select a small crystal or tumblestone for each of the chakra centres and place one at each centre with the exception of the crown chakra, which is your direct link with the source. It is advisable not to place any stones in direct contact with the physical crown of the head, but to place a small quartz or amethyst in the aura a few inches above the physical location. Create a room or personal grid in which to lie before you start. Small quartz points can be used with the other stones to link and move the energies.

The experienced practitioner might use a variety of stones in the chakra layout, always bearing in mind that not only do you and your client have a particular energy, but each of the stones you choose has its own energy. I have collected a wide range of small healing stones over the years, but I come back to a few crystals over and over again. Those I regularly use include: quartz, amethyst, celestite, azurite, lapis lazuli, fluorite, tourmaline, apopholite, kunzite, aquamarine, rose quartz, aventurine, jade, citrine, topaz, tiger's eye, carnelian, jasper, garnet, ruby, various agates and smoky and rutilated quartz. The interaction of different stones will also change the balance of energies you are setting up. Take care, be sensitive and keep it simple. Less is usually more in terms of effectiveness.

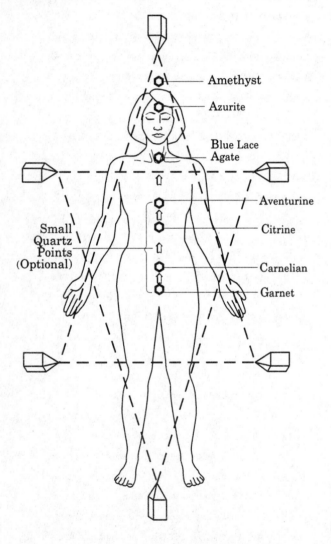

Illustration 4: Simple Sample Chakra Layout

CHAKRA BALANCE VISUALISATION

This is a wonderful visualisation exercise for balancing the chakras and is an extended version of the one given by Glen Park in her far-reaching book *The Art of Changing*. Unless you have a friend to lead you through it, record it on to a cassette tape so that you can relax and listen without the need to read. This exercise can be done with or without crystals. Ideally you should be lying or sitting within a balancing grid such as the Star of David (see page 34).

You may also use this exercise for a patient while they are receiving a treatment. I use this visualisation often; it is very relaxing and is a marvellous support to energy healing, as the minds of both healer and patient are reinforcing balance with colour, light and positive affirmations.

VISUALISATION MEDITATION

Start by getting settled and relaxed. Close your eyes and focus gently on your breathing. Centre yourself and watch your own breathing. Without strain, allow your breathing to settle into an easy, steady rhythm.

Now bring your awareness gently to the *base of the spine* and imagine a strong, clear *red* light. Think of a rich red sunset or the glow of ruby. Sense the quality of this red energy and as it brightens and glows send it spiralling outwards from the coccyx, filling your pelvis and right down your legs to your feet and toes. Say to yourself:

'I accept my instinctual nature, that part of me which is purely animal.'

Move your awareness up to your *sacrum* and imagine the light changing to a gentle *orange* like firelight, filling your lower abdomen and right across your belly. Sense the quality of that orange light — the energy is a little different from the red below. And say to yourself:

'I accept my emotional nature, my need for pleasure and nurturing.'

Moving up to your *solar plexus*, imagine a lovely *golden yellow* light, like the sun, filling your diaphragm, the whole of your upper abdomen filled with golden yellow sunlight. Say to yourself:

'I accept my power, my ability to succeed and my need to have some control over my life.'

Then bring the energy up to your *heart centre*, at the centre of your chest, and imagine the light becoming a pure, clear *green*. Imagine the hills and trees and sunlight through new spring leaves. See this lovely green filling your chest, round your shoulders and right down your arms to your fingertips. This is the green of new life, growth and healing. And say to yourself:

'I accept myself totally, exactly as I am now. I am.'

Now bring your awareness up to your *throat*, and see a clear, fresh, *sky blue* light filling your throat and extending to make a circle from the tips of your ears, taking in your nose, mouth, jaw and round to where your collar bones meet. Say to yourself:

'I accept the way I express myself in the world. I accept my creative nature.'

At your *brow*, now imagine a deep *indigo blue* light, like the night sky, extending out to fill the rest of your head, like deep space. Say to yourself:

'I accept my wisdom, my understanding of reality.'

Finally, at the *crown* of your head imagine a clear *violet* light pouring outwards, upwards, from the top of your head and finally imagine it dissolving into pure, brilliant white light as you say to yourself:

'I accept my divinity, my connection with cosmic, universal energy.'

You have now built all the colours of the spectrum of light. Each of these colours symbolises a different expression of the life force as it flows through you. Each is equally vital, important and interdependent. And just as when the colours are blended together they make light, so, when your energies are balanced and in harmony, you become a perfect channel for the life force, which you can visualise as white light.

Increase that life force now. Imagine a source of pure *white* light above the crown of your head and visualise it pouring down all around you, like a bright shower or sparkling waterfall. See the light growing brighter and brighter and feel it filling your aura, washing away all sadness, fear, pain and darkness. And imagine that you can draw it down into you through the crown of your head on your in-breath. *Breathe it into the centre of your being*, increasing your own inner light. On your out-breath, imagine that you are *sending the light to every cell and atom of your body*. See the whole of you, inside and out, radiant with the light; the life force energy. Continue to breathe quietly and circulate the light for a few minutes. Say to yourself:

'I am in the light and the light is in me.'

Allow yourself a few minutes to bathe and rest in the light before gently re-focusing on your breathing. Wiggle your hands and feet and gently open your eyes. If you have been lying on your back, roll over onto your side and rest in a foetal position for a few minutes before getting up.

QUARTZ PENDULUM DIAGNOSIS

Pendulums are a marvellous tool for the healing practitioner. They can be used for dowsing in diagnosis, for prescribing

remedies and for energy balancing as well as a multitude of
other purposes. A pendulum that is made from a natural
quartz point (or any other natural crystal) carries the
energetic properties of the crystal, which will influence its
function as a pendulum. For regular dowsing, it is best to use
an ordinary pendulum (made from wood or resin), especially
if you are just starting to develop your dowsing skills.

PENDULUM EXERCISE

Centre yourself, spine straight, shoulders relaxed and
breathing deeply from the belly. Hold the pendulum
lightly from the top of its cord or chain. Relax and tell
yourself that the pendulum will begin to turn
clockwise. Wait; do not consciously move your hand,
but just allow your unconscious to contact you through
the pendulum. It will seem to move on its own but
actually your hand moves it involuntarily, in
coordination with your unconscious mind. If it does not
move, deliberately start it off to get the feel of what you
want. Then stop and wait again for it to occur without
your conscious interference. I suggest you use a
clockwise direction for yes or positive(+) and anticlockwise for no or negative (-).

Where a quartz pendulum really comes into its own
is for diagnosing and balancing the energy flow through
the chakras. The technique I am about to give you was
taught to me by Stephanie Collins and I have used it
countless times with good results. It is a bit complicated
and I suggest you keep a simple chart for your notes
with a system that you will understand when referring
to it at a later date. You can photocopy the sample I
have laid out here, or adapt it to make one that better
suits your needs.

CHAKRA DIAGNOSIS CHART

Client's Name _____

Date of Diagnosis _____

Chakra	Output Energy Flow	Input Energy Flow
Base		
Sacrum		
Solar Plexus		
Heart		
Throat		
Brow		
Crown		

Key (e.g. √OK, √√ Good, √√√ Strong, – weak, – – very weak, etc.)

Other notes

Use a clean and well-balanced natural quartz
pendulum. To begin the diagnosis, relax and centre
yourself. It is vital that you have already determined the
pendulum's indications for yes (+) and no (-). Your client
should be lying on her back. Make sure she is relaxed and
warm enough.

Decide first that you are going to diagnose the
strength and quality of energy *output* from each of the
chakras. Next, move to a position where the pendulum is
directly above the base chakra and allow the chakra to
indicate the direction or flow of energy from that chakra,
clockwise or anticlockwise, plus or minus. This is
important, as the chakra above it will flow in the opposite
direction and so on, altering directions until you reach the
crown. When the time comes for you to work on the
input energy flow to the chakras, the directions will be the
opposite of that shown for *output*. This sounds
complicated, but if you think of alternating wheels
spinning in one direction for output and the other way for
input it should help you. The effect is an alternating flow
like the twin snakes which twine around the staff of
Hermes (the spine) in the symbol of the caduceus.

Back to the chart. If your pendulum told you the
base chakra output energy direction was clockwise or +,
note that on your chart. Now let the pendulum indicate
the strength and quality of the flow by the strength and
type of movement you get from the pendulum over the
base chakra. Other points to look out for might be
elliptical or irregular oscillating movements from the
pendulum, indicating imbalances. (Clearly you will need
to be comfortable and experienced with your pendulum
to do this work effectively.) Note your results on your
chart noting in the key section the way you are 'scoring'

'√' and '–' (minus) as I have suggested, or use a scale of 1–10. This is to facilitate making intelligent notes for yourself.

So if, for example, the base chakra indicates clockwise and strong, you will enter both these facts against Base/Output on the chart. Still working on output energy, move up to the sacrum, which you know will be anticlockwise if the base was clockwise. You need only to observe and record the quality and strength of the energy. Mark your chart. Move on to the solar plexus, which you know will be clockwise, and make your notes. Continue in this way right up to the crown.

When you are ready to determine input flow, begin again at the base chakra. You will know that if the direction for output was clockwise, then this time the pendulum will show anticlockwise for the input flow to that chakra, and the opposite of their output directions will be true for each of the other chakras also. When you have noted all the indications for both output and input energy flow to the chakras, assess your findings and move on to balancing any inharmonies you may have noted with your pendulum. This diagnosis may provide you with the basis for working on the underlying causes of imbalance in a therapeutic way (see Chapter Nine).

QUICK PENDULUM RE-BALANCING

To re-balance the energy in or out of a particular chakra, deliberately spin the pendulum strongly in the correct direction for the chakra's energy and let it continue until it comes to a complete rest directly over the chakra. The *exception* to this is the crown chakra, which I think is best not interfered with. This is because the spiritual balance and well-being of each of us is the concern of a higher principle; our higher self, the universal energy or God, whichever concept you find most comfortable. When you have made the corrections you think necessary to the other chakras, go back and check the chakras again with the pendulum in the way you made your original diagnosis to ensure they are all now well balanced.

While this method is very effective in the short term, it is no substitute for deeper work on the causes underlying any imbalances that show up. If these are tackled with sensitivity and integrity, a permanent healing can take place. You can also use the pendulum diagnosis as a prelude to a chakra balancing crystal and gemstone layout, or to assist you in choosing gem or flower remedies.

SAMPLE LAYOUTS

You will find that most books on crystal healing agree on basic healing layouts and only differ in the details. There is usually an overall containing or sacred space created by quartz crystals surrounding the patient. Within this grid, the layout depends on the desired treatment, but will generally be balancing the personal energy system by either calming and clearing or stimulating and boosting (see Illustrations 5 and 6).

Ten to fifteen minutes in a layout should be enough time to get results and I suggest you start by trying them yourself and carefully monitoring the effects. You will sense immediately if the choice and placement of the stones is wrong, as you may feel dizzy or slightly nauseated. Use your common sense and *keep it simple*; my teacher's motto was KISS (Keep it simple, stupid!). A few well chosen and well placed stones are far more effective than a complicated muddle of conflicting energies.

Note: The illustration samples are based on grids for individuals with right-sided polarities i.e. their energy flow is outwards on their right side. Reverse the hand and foot crystals for a left-sided flow.

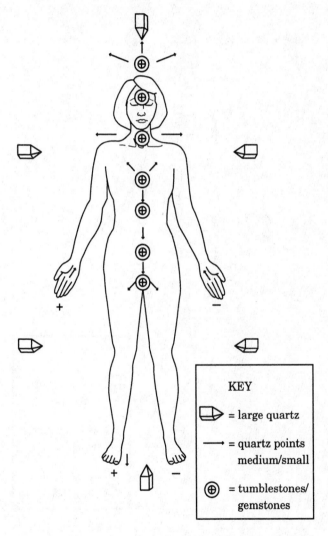

Illustration 5: Sample Clearing/Calming Grid Layout

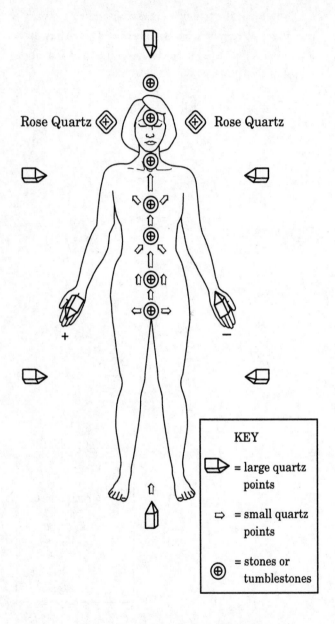

Illustration 6: Sample Boosting Grid

CHAPTER SEVEN

Crystal Dreaming

A part from their specific healing functions, crystals have an age-old reputation as tools for meditation, divination and dream work. The shamanic tradition provides us with some fascinating and effective techniques which we can adapt for personal use and in this chapter I will outline some of the ways crystals can support your spiritual growth and practice.

PREPARING FOR MEDITATION

Meditation is an ancient technique for quietening the everyday mind and looking within for peace, wisdom and guidance. Preparation is important and only the most adept can really attain a meditative state amidst noise, confusion and distraction. Try and find a space where you can be alone without interruption — if possible, keep a little room or even the corner of a room, specifically for meditation. First, thoroughly clean the space you have chosen. Next, use one of the crystal grids outlined in Chapter Four to create the appropriate energy. Whether you prefer a simple environment, or to decorate it with a few well-chosen objects, is a matter of personal choice. Flowers, candles, artwork, music, incense might inspire serenity in one but bring distraction to another.

It is also down to practical preference, whether you sit cross-legged on the floor (or in a half or full lotus, for the yoga practitioner) or in an upright chair. It is important to choose a sitting position which you can comfortably maintain for between half and three quarters of an hour. Your spine should be straight and supported.

A chair, which is the best choice for most people, should
be straight-backed, without arms and of average height,
allowing you to have both feet hip-width apart and flat
on the floor, with knees bent at 90°. Legs are best
uncrossed, as energy can then move freely and you have
good contact with the ground. (Sitting on the ground
with a straight spine will give a similar 'grounding', as
the base chakra is in contact with the ground.) Your
shoulders should be relaxed, arms comfortably by your
sides and your hands resting in your lap.

When you are ready to begin, turn off the phone
and anything else that might interrupt you. Check your
body for muscle tension, especially neck, shoulders and
buttocks. To relax tight muscles, tense the affected areas
even more tightly, hold until it's uncomfortable, then
release completely. Next, use your breathing. Establish an
easy rhythm, slow but comfortable, and allow yourself to
observe your breathing for a few minutes as your busy
mind quietens. If you find distracting thoughts flitting into
your mind, just allow the thoughts to float past, as if on an
inner screen, and then off again. This peaceful non-
anxiety will settle you better than any amount of effort.
Trying to meditate, to let go or to push away thoughts,
is always counter-productive.

CRYSTAL TEACHERS AND INNER JOURNEYS

The first meditation given here is one I use often and it
is based on the meditation given by Pamela Chase and
Jonathan Pawlik in *The Newcastle Guide to Healing with
Crystals*. Unless you have a friend to read for you, record
the meditations on to a cassette which you can play back.
The key is to relax and take it slowly, allowing good
long pauses between each line of the meditation.

ENTERING THE CRYSTAL

Sit upright and make sure you are warm, comfortable and relaxed. Remember, it is best to have your legs uncrossed and placed flat on the ground or floor. Hold your crystal in your receiving hand, or in both hands, and allow yourself to become quiet and receptive, breathing regularly and slowly.

With thoughts of pure love and light ask your crystal to open an area of its structure so you may enter its perfect form

See your crystal make a special space for you

Enter your crystal through the doorway of light provided for you

Feeling in a state of perfect balance, choose to explore the interior of your crystal

Allow all your senses to be open to experience your crystal

Touch its sides, its foundation, with your face, your hands

Allow your body to lean against a crystal wall

Listen to any sounds you may hear

Feel you are at home and totally welcomed by your crystal

Spend a little while enjoying the attunement

Now prepare to leave

Thank your crystal for sharing its energies with you

Re-focus on your breathing, wiggle your hands and feet and return to the present

Open your eyes.

The above meditation can be used in a lot of ways. It is a fundamental tool in deep crystal work and it provides a good basis for further meditations you can devise yourself. As a teaching meditation, you can enter the crystal with the intention of receiving help with a problem. Or when you are inside the crystal you might ask for guidance, advice or a new perspective on a particular issue that concerns you. This may be essentially practical or of a spiritual nature, in which case it provides a lovely focus for personal development. Meeting the Wise Teacher (see below) is a meditation that takes you into the crystal as a sacred place for actually meeting your inner guide.

Another use for this form of meditation is as a starting point for journey work, using the crystal as a doorway to another level of reality. This may be seen as a form of astral travelling; the reason a quartz crystal provides such a wonderful doorway is because crystals are one of the few substances with the same appearance on the physical level as on the inner levels. Because of this, crystals have been invaluable to shamans the world over, accessing non-ordinary reality and the dreamtime.

MEETING THE WISE TEACHER

Sit upright and make sure you are warm, comfortable and relaxed. It is best to have your legs uncrossed and placed flat on the ground or floor. Hold your crystal and allow yourself to become quiet and receptive, breathing regularly and slowly.

With thoughts of pure love and light ask your crystal to open an area of its structure so you may enter its perfect form

See your crystal make a special space for you

Enter your crystal through the doorway of light provided for you

Feeling in a state of perfect balance, choose to explore the interior of your crystal

Allow all your senses to be open to experience your crystal

Touch its sides, its foundation, with your face,
your hands

Allow your body to lean against a crystal wall

Listen to any sounds you may hear

Feel you are at home and totally welcomed by
your crystal

Now ask your wise teacher to appear to you

Become aware of a shining figure approaching

Feel the energy of pure love radiating from this figure

You know it is your guide or wise teacher

Find a place where you can sit together and enjoy
this sacred meeting

Enjoy the attunement with this being who knows
and loves you completely

Share the heartfelt matters of your soul, for
several minutes

Now, bid farewell, knowing you will meet again
many times — indeed, you are never really apart

Prepare to leave

Thank your crystal for providing this sacred
meeting place

Re-focus on your breathing, wiggle your hands
and feet and return to the present

Open your eyes.

ENTERING THE DREAMTIME

Sit upright and make sure you are warm, comfortable and
relaxed. It is best to have your legs uncrossed and placed
flat on the ground or floor. Hold your crystal and allow
yourself to become quiet and receptive, breathing
regularly and slowly.

With thoughts of pure love and light ask your crystal to
open an area of its structure so you may enter its perfect form

See your crystal make a special space for you

Enter your crystal through the doorway of light provided for you

Feeling in a state of perfect balance, choose to explore the interior of your crystal

Allow all your senses to be open to experience your crystal

Touch its sides, its foundation, with your face, your hands

Allow your body to lean against a crystal wall

Listen to any sounds you may hear

Feel you are at home and totally welcomed by your crystal

When you are ready, look for a silvery pathway or sparkling stream of water

Follow it until you reach a crystal cave

Go through the cave and emerge into a completely new and beautiful landscape

Spend several minutes exploring this new world

Now, prepare to return to your crystal cave

Do not bring anything back with you from this otherworldly journey

Re-experience the interior of the crystal

When you feel settled and centred, prepare to leave

Thank your crystal for providing a sacred doorway

Re-focus on your breathing, wiggle your hands and feet and return to the present

Open your eyes.

The reason for the instruction not to bring anything out with you is that it can create a link with the astral world which may sometimes give rise to troublesome intrusions in your everyday life.

MOVING MEDITATIONS

The Spiral of Nine layout (see page 36 and Illustration 2
for details) is a wonderful basis for a 'moving meditation'
and is best used outdoors or in a room where there is
enough space for you to walk the spiral in meditation,
with a chair (place the centre crystal point upwards
beneath) or cushion (sit cross-legged, with the centre
crystal held in both hands in your lap, point upwards)
at the centre. This spiral form is very powerful and will
quite radically alter your perceptions. As you move slowly
along the pathway to the centre you seem to travel a vast
distance and lose all sense of time. When you reach the
centre, you will become the meeting node of the upper
and lower worlds and the eye which sees through to other
realms of reality. When you are ready, make your way out
of the spiral clockwise, bringing the wisdom or awareness
you have contacted out with you into the world.

Remember that the choice of crystals and the
direction they are facing will influence the effect of the
spiral. For a very strong focus to the centre, using quartz
points, place the crystals facing anticlockwise along the
path of the spiral towards the centre. For a gentler and
more dispersing energy, place the crystal points clockwise.
Or place them all turned towards the centre or all rayed
outwards. Experiment and see which suits you best. A
gentler grid could be made using lumps of rough rose
quartz. Another variation is to use clusters or a cluster at
the centre, or a combination of any of these.

SPIRAL OF RETURN AND REBIRTH
Energy flows in spirals, circular and wavelike — like
the tides of life

The sea

The moon

The seasons

Ebb and flow

All are born, expand, contract, re-form

Active and passive by turns

The spiral becomes also the double spiral of your
own DNA

As you move to the centre

And out again with a new awareness.

As you move very slowly and deliberately, anticlockwise through the spiral, the world begins to dissolve

And you are at the centre

Take your seat at the heart of creation, where all
worlds meet

And all is one time

No time

Here

And nowhere — which is to say you are now here.

You are at the centre of creation

The eye of the whirlwind

The centre of a spinning galaxy of shining stars

The tiny spiral shell

Where all possibility is born

Be here now, for several minutes

Until you make your return

Out to the place where you started but seeing as if
for the first time

From a new perspective

Reborn!

THE SPIRAL INITIATION

Because of the deep effect the spiral form has on the
mind, it is a very suitable grid to use as the basis for

ceremonial. I have found it especially effective to blindfold the initiate and to guide them slowly to the centre where you help them to sit and attune with their new state of being and to receive their initiation on the inner levels. The guide leads them carefully back out again at the appropriate time. In spiritual group work, this can be a very special focus for the beginning or end of the gathering. Work in pairs, one to assist the other, allowing each member a turn at the centre.

CRYSTAL DREAMTIME

Crystals will amplify your ability to dream. In the native American tradition, herkimer diamonds (see Directory, page 105) are used as dream stones for their protection while sleeping and to help the remembering of dreams. They are especially good for people who do not remember their dreams at all, as the herkimer always assists balance by bringing into consciousness the opposite of your present awareness. For dream work, the herkimer should be cleansed well in spring water with a sprinkling of sea salt in it before you start and then every time you use it. You can hold the herkimer in your hand while you sleep, or place it under your pillow.

A rose quartz under the pillow will help with dream recall as well as helping to stop nightmares. You should cleanse the crystal in the usual way, attune yourself to the individual nature of the crystal and then inform it clearly and respectfully that you wish to be helped to remember your dreams or protected from nightmares.

In the Sun Bear book, *Dreaming with the Wheel* (see Recommended Reading, page 119), Shawnodese tells the story of a Salish tribal elder, who in old age developed crippling arthritis which prevented her from the travelling

she had formerly so much enjoyed. Her daughter shared
this love of travel and would bring back to her mother a
tiny stone from any special place she had visited. The elder
would then sleep with this little stone and dream not only
of the place her daughter had visited, but of what had
happened when her daughter was there. This technique
is a sort of 'dream psychometry' and implies some
interesting possible uses.

DREAM MEETINGS

One variation of the technique described above can be
used to effect dream meetings between separated loved
ones. The two friends or lovers exchange personal
crystals on parting then hold the beloved's crystal as
they fall asleep, perhaps also bringing to mind the
person's image.

LUCID CRYSTAL DREAMING

This is a technique which might interest you if you want
to encourage lucid dreams. Use your personal crystal —
that is, one you know extremely well. I recommend you
do the Entering the Crystal meditation described on page
65, to effect a close link with the crystal as a preparation
for this approach to lucid dreaming.

   Knowing that crystals have the same structure in the
dream world as they do in waking reality, you can hold
and connect with your crystal on falling asleep, with the
conscious intention of looking for it in your dream state.
When you find your crystal it will be a signal to you that
you are dreaming and you will 'go lucid'. The real trick is
to hold a lucid dream, which takes practice and familiarity.
When it first happens, if you are anything like me, you get
over-excited and wake up!

CHAPTER EIGHT

Gem Elixirs

Gem elixirs are made from spring water charged with specific crystals and gemstones. They are especially good for treating negative mental and emotional states and where healing requires changing long-term, ingrained attitudes and conditioning. The effect can be subtle, and so it can be hard to be sure the changes are directly due to the essence. With practice, you can learn to feel the presence of the essence and differentiate the effects of the different gems. Gem elixirs are outside the Medicines Act in the UK, which states that it is illegal to claim that a product is beneficial in treating a physical ailment without it having undergone successful clinical trials and the subsequent granting of a licence.

MAKING GEM ELIXIRS
WHAT YOU NEED
- crystals and gemstones, preferably in their natural state
- spring or distilled water
- glass jars or glasses
- brandy
- glass dropper bottles, sterilised in boiling water
- labels

After you have cleaned and charged your gemstones (see Chapter Three), you can make gem water (also called structured water) or gem essence (also called tinctures, remedies and elixirs). This is an excellent way to learn about the gemstones and to discover how the stones work with your own energies. The properties of the individual stones will give you some idea of how the essences might

work. Keep a record of how you are feeling when you are
taking a gem essence and any changes that occur. Learn
about the effects of the gem elixirs on yourself before
giving them to anyone else.

METHOD

Place the cleansed stone in an empty, sterilised glass jar or
glass. If you are making gem water, use a large jar such as a
pickling jar. You can use something much smaller for
essences. Add spring or distilled water. Cover the container
(with glass ideally) and place it on a natural surface (grass,
earth, wood) outside in the sun for several hours or, even
better, for 24 hours at full moon to get the benefit of sun
and moon. Moon energies are very good for emotional
healing. Bless the water in the way you feel most
comfortable. For example, say a favourite prayer of
thanksgiving, or tune in to the nature spirits (Devas),
asking their help in charging the water for healing.

Gem water lasts for about three days at most. If you
wish to use the remedy on an ongoing basis, you must
preserve it as an essence as follows:

Sterilise a brown dropper bottle (with glass dropper),
usually available from your local pharmacy. Then fill the
bottle halfway with the gem water. Fill the rest of the
bottle with brandy. Now you have an essence which is
50 per cent water and 50 per cent alcohol. Label the bottle
as 'stock', e.g. 'ruby stock', and store on a shelf out of the
sunlight. If you have made several different waters, store
them so that the bottles are not touching.

Take the essence either by putting 5 drops from the
stock into a glass of spring water and sip at intervals
through the day. Or make up another dropper bottle of
the essence to carry with you, as follows:

Sterilise another dropper bottle and fill one third full of brandy. Top up with spring water and add 2–5 drops of your stock and shake. Label it to differentiate it from your stock. Take drops under your tongue, or in water. If you re-use bottles, sterilise them well, especially the droppers. Boiling for 20 minutes is good practice. Little and often is the best way of dosing. You can become overcharged with gem essences — signs such as spaciness or dizziness will let you know you should stop.

Bear in mind that you should use gem waters only if treating someone who is not taking alcohol.

WHEN TO USE GEM ELIXIRS
GEM ELIXIRS FOR MENTAL AND EMOTIONAL STATES

Take the elixir in the same way you might take a flower essence — in water or as drops on your tongue. The dosage should be little and often. Make a careful note of any changes you feel and stop if you feel spacy or out of balance. The use of vibrational essences is a subtle art and a responsible and sensitive approach will bring rewarding results. For specific gem elixir indications, consult the Directory, pages 87-112. For a detailed and excellent reference work, consult Gurudas' *Gem Elixirs and Vibrational Healing*.

GEM ELIXIRS AND CRYSTALS

You can modify the charge in your crystals with gem elixirs. For example, putting a drop or two of rose quartz elixir on to a clear quartz pendant, or into a clean basin of water in which you soak the crystal, will bring the vibration of rose quartz into the aura when the pendant is worn, energised by the clear quartz. This approach is useful in self-development work, where you might feel the need of different energetic influences at different stages of your process.

ENVIRONMENTAL AND AURA CLEANSING WITH GEM ELIXIRS

Gem elixirs will also modify any crystals used in environmental and healing layouts. A crystal gem water which you spray in the environment (a plant mister is good for this) will bring energy to the atmosphere. Plants particularly love to be misted with gem water if they are ailing. Water is an excellent carrier of subtle energy. Gem elixirs can be effectively added to your bath to bring the vibrational influence into your aura.

PENDULUM DIAGNOSIS

Pendulum diagnosis is useful when choosing essences for clients. First dose yourself with an essence that balances you and releases your personal will (try quartz or tourmalated quartz). Hold the client's sending hand in your receiving hand, relax and affirm you are seeking an essence for the person's highest good at this time. Then dowse for the correct essence or essences needed and the quantities and times of dosing. If you do not have experience with a pendulum, see the pendulum exercise on page 56. Confidence will come with practice.

Alcohol, coffee and cigarettes can reduce the effectiveness of the remedies, so do not follow a dose of essence with a coffee or a cigarette. Instead, work with the essence, affirming its qualities and benefits to you in a mini-meditation. Unlike flower essences, gem essences can interfere with homeopathic remedies, so check with your homeopath if appropriate.

CHAPTER NINE

Complementary Crystals

In my practice I use massage with the majority of my clients. Massage has a great many benefits to mind, body and emotions and makes an ideal preliminary to a crystal healing, a chakra balance or crystal journey work. The physical benefits of massage have been long recognised — it improves blood circulation, skin and muscle tone and it benefits the digestive and lymphatic systems. It can also be very enjoyable, bringing comfort and a non-threatening touch.

Deep tissue massage can ease muscle spasms and can help heal muscular injuries. It can also work at an emotional level to release trauma that has been locked into the musculature of the body. This form of psycho-therapeutic massage has been developed into a very effective therapy in its own right, thanks to the pioneering work of such figures as Wilhelm Reich and Ida Rolfe.

Massage is deeply relaxing and as a de-stressor it can hardly be bettered except, perhaps, with the addition of crystals. Having soft, freed muscles (often for the first time in months or even years) allows the whole system to let go, bringing a marvellous sense of well-being and peace. The increased energy that is felt after a good massage can be enormous, as it costs a lot of energy to keep going when we're holding on to pain by tensing our muscles.

The masseur can use crystals in the treatment room both as a room grid to create a sacred working space (see pages 27-38) and by using a quartz grid, such as the Star of David, described on page 33, around the massage couch.

Other options include a good clear quartz or amethyst cluster or a large lump of natural rose quartz, or spheres of any of these crystals, placed in the room to bring a sense of clarity and well-being to the environment.

AROMATHERAPY

Massage with scented oils delights the senses, but in aromatherapy the effects of the oils go far beyond sensual pleasure and can treat a wide variety of ailments with excellent results. This is due to the effect of the oils on the nervous system and the balance of the brain. This specialist area has become far more widely practised recently and it is hard to imagine a more pleasant way of being treated for conditions as wide-ranging as migraine to a difficult menopause. As with most therapies, the efficacy of the treatment depends largely on the skill and sensitivity of the practitioner and the receptivity of the client.

The aromatherapist can use crystals in the treatment room as described above. She can also experiment with the effects of energising the oils with crystals, either by placing quartz crystal in the store cupboard, or by actually putting a small crystal or tumblestone in the treatment oil itself. This approach should produce some interesting affinities and I would be very glad to hear of any results from aromatherapists who might try it.

CRYSTALS AND REFLEXOLOGY

Reflexology is another effective therapy, which treats the organs of the body via zones on the feet and, sometimes, the hands. Not only is it excellent as a treatment for a variety of physical conditions — especially when other treatments may be too invasive or just unsuitable — it is also an excellent means of diagnosis.

A crystal grid around the patient might be used to balance the energy field, enhancing the receptivity of the patient to the healing. The patient could also hold a crystal on the part of the physical body which is being treated on the foot. In certain cases, the therapist might consider using a small quartz point to treat specific zonal points.

CRYSTALS AND HERBS

The healing use of herbs is an intrinsic part of eastern medicine and it also underpins much of traditional medicine in the west. Much of our modern pharmacopoeia is derived from the more ancient lore of herbs and their healing properties. Crystals can be used effectively in conjunction with herbal remedies in many cases where you wish to treat energetically as well as physically.

CRYSTALS AND SOUND

Sound is energy waves which send out a vibrational resonance through space. It is not difficult to believe that the myriad vibrations of the living universe, in all its diverse expressions, might be the same essence that is referred to as the music of the spheres. The power of certain sounds and chanting have been an important part of the inner practice of all the great world religions. We know, too, that listening to baroque music has particular effects on the brainwaves — it can accelerate learning — and that certain types of dissonant music can cause mental disturbance.

Because crystals and sound both work on the vibrational level, they can interact with powerful effect. Some therapists work by toning certain vowel sounds and notes through crystals to cause far-reaching energetic

changes. This is a specialist area which goes beyond the
bounds of this book — you can occasionally find courses
and workshops in therapeutic sound.

CRYSTALS AND PSYCHOTHERAPY

Often when a client comes to me for counselling or
psychotherapy, I will give them a lump of rose quartz to
hold to ease the stress of painful memories. Even this
simple contact can comfort and soothe, bringing a
welcome release of pent-up emotions. One woman, who
was very sensitive, used a quartz point to locate areas in
her body where she felt pressure and a heavy blackness.
By holding the crystal she was able to create images to
express her pain, which we then unravelled together.
The crystal continued to pull out images, until at last she
felt clear and light, tired, but free of the oppressive feelings
that had been overwhelming her.

Different crystals can be used in counselling
situations, depending on the need. In the examples just
given, the effect of clear quartz was probing — drawing
out toxic thoughts and feelings — whereas rose quartz
was used to soothe and ease. Holding and tuning in to a
phantom quartz crystal can assist in pulling out repeating
patterns and distant memories (and even images which
present as 'past lives'). An amethyst can help with
destructive habits and addictive behaviour; a fluorite
can bring a balance to brain functions that helps clear
thinking when sorting out problems.

These are just some of the ways crystals can enhance
other therapeutic methods. At the very least, a good
balancing crystal grid in the therapy room (see Chapter
Four) is beneficial to both the practitioner and the patient,
as it creates a balanced energy field in which to work.

CHAPTER TEN

Crystals, Pets, Plants and People

B y now you will have realised that healing with crystals does not take a cookbook approach. By this I mean: for sore toe apply this gemstone, for headache, that one — although there are crystals which will have a beneficial influence in a variety of acute conditions (that is, when the ailment is recent and has not had a long time to become fixed and complex). In the Directory on pages 87-112, you will find the major crystals and gemstones listed with their traditional therapeutic associations. It is useful to acquaint yourself with these and, even more importantly, to take time out to explore the influence of individual stones for yourself.

But how will you know when crystals might help? The ways are indeed many and varied, as crystals can be used to affect anything with an energy field. Trial and error is fine, as long as you remember to apply the basic principles of cleanliness, balance and respectfulness. Also, it is essential that you do not interfere with or try to undermine any other treatment that may be being given. So before you start, always make sure that you and your crystals are as clean and as energetically clear as possible.

As humans, we have very fine faculties of reason, intuition and understanding but sometimes we have difficulty applying them in a balanced way. If you cut yourself, the *first thing* you do is clean and dress the wound. You *do not* reach for the crystals while you bleed to death! It seems elementary to make this point, but often people get so carried away with a particular approach that they become blind to the obvious.

CRYSTALS TO TREAT ACUTE ILLNESS

Examples of acute conditions which may be relieved by
crystals are manifold. A toothache can often be soothed by
holding a little piece of jade against the tooth. A muscular
strain can be helped using clear quartz to ease the pain and
reduce inflammation. A dog had a damaged hind-leg that
was skillfully treated by the vet. But as the injury began to
heal, the dog worried at the leg and risked re-opening the
wound. Gentle passes with quartz crystal helped to 'draw
off' the irritation and calmed the dog, so that he allowed
the wound to heal without further interference.

When John first came to see me, he suffered from
regular bouts of severe sinus pain and pressure headaches.
I treated him with crystals for the pain. The first treatment
brought immediate relief and lasted about a week. After
two more treatments the sinus condition had not recurred,
except once, when John was very emotionally stressed by
an impending business dispute. The emotional cause of his
physical ill-health is part of a larger picture which we are
still unravelling, but crystals can be invaluable in treating
acute symptoms along the way. To treat John's sinus,
within a Star of David grid I used a small quartz point on
either side of his head, pointed away from his temples, to
draw off the pressure, two pieces of jade placed on either
side of his nose and a fluorite octahedron on his brow to
further assist in clearing up the condition.

CRYSTALS AND PLANTS

It is not only people and animals that respond so well to
crystals. A plant that has stopped thriving when you have
checked all obvious physical causes can often be revived by
placing a little piece of rose quartz in the earth at its roots.
A quartz cluster beside a sickly pot plant can work wonders

and a few drops of moss agate or quartz gem elixir in the watering can will give all your plants a boost. Vegetables watered in this way will thrive and be full of flavour. A few tumblestones in the bottom of a glass vase will not only look pretty but will extend the life of the flowers too. The implication is clear — the crystal influences the energy field, whether it be in plant, animal or person.

CRYSTALS TO BOOST ENERGY

Crystals can be particularly helpful in conditions where the immune system is depressed and where the symptoms are energetic, mental and emotional. This frequently involves extreme tiredness, random aches and pains, cramps, depression, anxiety, fear and poor sleep patterns. As already mentioned elsewhere in the book, the ME sufferer, for example, can often benefit from crystals, because the strengthening of the energy field will give the patient sufficient strength to tackle the bigger issue — why the illness has manifested at this time. In the case of all illness, this is a question that needs to be asked, at the appropriate time. Otherwise, the implication is that we are at the mercy of apparently random attacks of pain, illness and misfortune.

HOLISTIC HEALING

This approach is far from straightforward or simplistic and lies at the very heart of all holistic healing practices. The underlying reasons for one man's heart attack might include: stress caused by overwork, because that is what he learnt from his father, who in turn overworked and neglected his wife, who felt unloved and turned to her son for emotional support, who developed a weight problem due to comfort eating, which eventually dangerously raised his cholesterol and led to a heart attack.

Treating the acute condition, while essential in the example given, is no guarantee against the condition recurring. The example itself is fiction, created to illustrate the complexity of imbalances — of belief, environment and behaviour — that can give rise to illness. It is for this reason that I rarely treat a serious condition purely with crystals, and often recommend other approaches in tandem with my treatment — there will be someone with just the right skills to assist the healing process further if the patient really desires to be helped.

CRYSTALS AND CONSCIOUSNESS

The work of the holistic practitioner is very often to help her client to ask the important questions and to support the client's quest for self-knowledge and subsequent self-healing. Like placing pieces of a delicate puzzle, the individual's true potential is gradually seen and its beauty emerges. Crystals can assist with this process of consciousness. A good crystal layout in the hands of a sensitive therapist can unblock energy, free buried and painful memories, and help the client see patterns of meaning, all in the context of a balanced and protected space. Experience has shown me that crystals have a place in deep healing work of this kind, in what are essentially soul matters.

Mary came to me when she was going through the final stages of separation from her husband of twenty-five years. She was confused and exhausted, unable to sleep without medication, depressed and at times almost suicidal. The breakdown of the marriage was reflected in the breakdown of her being. She felt she had no separate existence or identity outside the marriage — it had been the container for her sense of purpose and self-worth.

Using crystals to clear and re-balance her aura
calmed her and paved the way for the deep work which
followed. Mary needed to discover a sense of meaning
in her life that did not depend on her circumstances
remaining fixed and unchanged. Her healing journey,
via bodywork, counselling, crystal meditations and re-
balancing took her back to destructive patterns established
in childhood (and earlier ancestral echoes). She was a girl
— the girls helped mother and served father and sons —
and her musical talent went unremarked and
unsupported.

Gradually new insights emerged into ways in which
these patterns played out in her relationship with her
husband and children and ultimately she was able to stop
judging and start loving herself — she has now taken
up the piano again and her lessons take priority.
Unravelling requires support, careful rebuilding and
establishing something better. Crystals can assist changes
and ultimately lead to transformations. For an inspiring
account of the vital importance a sense of connectedness
and meaning has in our lives, I suggest you read Thomas
Moore's *Care of the Soul*.

One of the most difficult realisations can be that
healing does not necessarily mean preventing death.
One of the greatest gifts of healing is the conscious
preparation for death and moving on. Sogyal Rinpoche's
The Tibetan Book of Living and Dying is a practical guide to
making our dying as conscious and loving as we make
our living. Drawing on the great tradition of Tibetan
Buddhism, he shows how to acknowledge death as an
ever-present reality and describes a way of being in
the present moment that is clear, wise and infinitely
compassionate.

CONTRA-INDICATIONS

When treating with crystals, be sensitive to possible
contra-indications for certain conditions. During
pregnancy, astonishing energy transformations are taking
place and the energetic harmony of the mother at all levels
is of paramount importance. Do not place any crystals
directly on the belly of a pregnant woman, especially in
the first trimester. If you wish to use crystals, be sure that
their influence is gentle, comforting and life-affirming.
I often recommend rose quartz as a helpful gift for
expectant mothers, women in labour and new babies,
as it is non-invasive and supportive.

The energy system of a newborn infant is extremely
delicate and it takes years to become fully adapted to
the rough and ready mix of energies that surround us
all the time. So gentle protection of the young aura is
helpful, but interference with a naturally developing
awareness and immunity is not. All developing life needs
unconditional love and respect. When in doubt, don't
interfere.

Cancers and other growths should also be treated
with care. Healers should not direct energy at the disease,
as there is a possibility you may 'feed' it. Instead, focus on
creating a balanced energy field, a strong connection with
the life force (see the Visualisation Meditation on page 43)
and on any insights the patient may have about the
underlying causes of the disease. In chronic conditions
where the patient is very fragile, it is best to heal at the
subtlest levels only, essentially aligning their spiritual
essence with the life force. Visualise the patient in the
gentle protection of the Light. Seeing them filled and
well and surrounded with pure pearly-white light will
be helpful in supporting their spiritual connection.

Directory

This Directory is an alphabetically organised ready reference for the most popular gemstones and crystals used in healing. It lists their main sources worldwide, their hardness, specific gravity and the crystal system to which they belong. It also details their uses, historical associations and their healing properties, with a note about elixirs where relevant.

GROUP

A group is given in the listing below where the stone is part of a larger group category — for example, the quartz group, which is the most widely used in healing, has many members which share common characteristics but vary in colour (and therefore in energy/vibration) according to the addition of different trace elements. A specific example of this is amethyst, which is purple due to traces of iron.

HARDNESS

A crystal's hardness depends on how strongly the atoms are held together. A scale of hardness relating to all minerals is known as Mohs' Scale. Taking ten minerals as standards, he arranged them in order of hardness so that one mineral could only scratch those below it on the scale. The scale goes from 1 to 10, based on talc as the softest (1), gypsum (2), calcite (3), fluorite (4), apatite (5), orthoclase (6), quartz (7), topaz (8), corundrum (9) and diamond as the hardest (10). This is a relative scale. Diamond is, in fact, many times harder than talc.

SPECIFIC GRAVITY

The specific gravity, or relative density, of a crystal reflects the way the atoms are packed together. It is defined as the weight per unit volume — a crystal's weight compared to that of an equal volume of distilled water. To calculate specific gravity (SG), take the weight of the crystal in air (W1) and its weight in water (W2). W1 divided by W1 minus W2 gives you the specific gravity.

CRYSTAL SYSTEMS

Crystal systems refer to symmetry, which depends on a crystal's internal structure and the arrangement of atoms within it. If a crystal can be divided so that each half is the mirror image of the other, the dividing line is called the plane of symmetry. There are seven main systems.

DISTINGUISHING FEATURES OF CRYSTALS		
CLASSIFICATION	SHAPE AND ORIENTATION OF AXIS	FORM
ISOMETRIC/ CUBIC		Three axes of the same length and at right angles to each other.
TETRAGONAL		Three axes at right angles to each other. Two on the same plane of equal length, the third is perpendicular to them. Four- or eight-sided prisms and pyramid shapes.
HEXAGONAL		Three of the four axes are in a single plane radiating equally from the centre. The fourth axis is perpendicular to, and a different length from, the others. Six-sided shapes.

DISTINGUISHING FEATURES OF CRYSTALS		
CLASSIFICATION	SHAPE AND ORIENTATION OF AXIS	FORM
TRIGONAL		Similar to hexagonal. Parallel to the long axis there are three planes of symmetry.
ORTHORHOMBIC		Three unequal axes at right angles to one another. Shapes include variations on the pyramid form.
MONOCLINIC		Prism has inclined top and bottom faces. Three unequal axes, two at right angles to each other and the third at an incline to the other plane. Shapes are prism like.
TRICLINIC		Three unequal axes all at three different angles to each other. Three pairs of faces. Shapes with much less symmetry than shown in other six crystals systems.

Illustration 7: Distinguishing Features of Crystals

AGATE

Group: Quartz. *Location:* India, Brazil, Uruguay, USA, Canada, Germany and Russia. *Hardness:* 6½–7. *Specific Gravity:* 2.6. *Crystal System:* Hexagonal. A variety of chalcedony, agate is a banded microcrystalline quartz. The bands are usually shades of the same colour, but can be multicoloured, although often dyed for decorative purposes. *Properties:* Often called the 'fire stone', agate

imparts a sense of strength and courage. A powerful
healer, helping the digestion, lymph system, circulation
and pulses, it is thought to be earthing and energetic.
As *Elixir:* fire agate: For courage and discrimination,
especially in practical and material concerns; moss agate:
to assist plant care and growth and to strengthen a
connection with nature.

AMAZONITE (AMAZON STONE)

Group: Feldspar. *Location*: Brazil, Australia, India, Russia,
Madagascar, Namibia, Zimbabwe and USA. *Hardness*:
6–6½. *Specific Gravity*: 2.56–2.58. *Crystal System*: Triclinic.
Takes its name from the Amazon River, from which it was
believed the crystals flowed. Mostly light green, but
sometimes bluish or blue-green, these squat crystals often
have a mottled appearance and are semi-opaque. *Properties*:
Soothing to the nervous system; aligns the heart and
solar plexus chakras. Good for balancing the subtle
bodies and for assisting in letting go of harmful
tendencies, giving freedom to creative expression. As
Elixir: Helps assimilation of the life force and enhances
the effects of most other vibrational remedies.

AMETHYST

Group: Quartz. *Location*: Spectacular examples found in
Minas Gerais (Brazil); also, Australia, India, Sri Lanka,
Russia, Madagascar, South Africa, Czechoslovakia, USA
and Canada. *Hardness*: 7. *Specific Gravity*: 2.63–2.65.
Crystal System: Hexagonal. Derives its name from the
Greek *amethustos*, meaning 'not drunk' — as it was
believed the wearer was protected from the effects of
alcohol. The most precious of the quartz group of crystals
and highly prized as a gemstone. These violet, purple or

pink crystals always grow from a base. Colouring due to traces of iron, distributed in varying bands distinguishing amethyst from other similar crystals. *Properties*: Strengthens the immune and endocrine systems. Very powerful energiser and blood cleanser. Positively affects right brain activity and the pituitary and pineal glands. Representing the violet ray of alchemical transformation, it enhances psychism, aids meditation and gives strong protection when worn. As *Elixir*: Brings balance, integration and confidence. Enhances intuition and assists meditation.

AQUAMARINE

Group: Beryl. *Location*: Occurs in all continents; best gem-quality stones from Madagascar, Afghanistan, Russia, Brazil and USA. *Hardness*: 7½–8. *Specific Gravity*: 2.7. *Crystal System*: Hexagonal. Name derives from Latin and means 'water from the sea'; sailors traditionally carried aquamarine for good luck. Varies in colour from pale blue to light green. The bluer the crystal the more highly prized the stone, although light blue crystals can be heated to deepen their colour. Distinguished from topaz and spinel by its lustre and lack of grey or violet hue. *Properties*: Serene and cooling. Helps to banish fears and phobias. Useful for detoxifying the body and reducing fluid retention, it is also thought to cure motion sickness. As *Elixir*: Inspires and stimulates creativity and self-expression. Amplified results when combined with turquoise.

AVENTURINE

Group: Quartz. *Location*: Brazil, Australia, India, Nepal and Russia. *Hardness*: 7. *Specific Gravity*: 2.63–2.65. *Crystal System*: Hexagonal. Variety of crystalline quartz with sparkling mica inclusions. Name is from the Italian *avventura*, meaning 'chance', due to the accidental discovery of a spangled glass. *Properties*: In ancient Tibet, aventurine was used for near-sightedness. Centring, soothing and tranquilising. Eases fear and anxiety. Purifies subtle bodies, strengthens blood and improves elasticity of muscle tissue. Effective in treating skin diseases. As *Elixir*: For fearfulness. Useful in treating psychosomatic illness and in psychotherapy for helping to release past trauma.

AZURITE (CHESSYLITE)

Location: Chessy (France), Greece, Australia, Iran, Namibia, Mexico and Chile. *Hardness*: 3½–4. *Specific Gravity*: 3.7–3.9. *Crystal System*: Monoclinic. A copper ore from which azure (blue) pigment was first derived. It forms at lower temperatures than malachite, which it can turn into through ion exchange in moisture. Crystals are usually azure-blue, but can also be dark blue with a hint of green. Relatively soft, with a vitreous lustre. Powdered azurite will become greenish in time as it turns to malachite. *Properties*: Because of its copper content, azurite enhances the energy flow through the nervous system. It strengthens the blood and helps the body to utilise oxygen. Inspiring creativity, azurite helps cut though illusion, cleanses the mental body and enhances meditation. Can also ease arthritis and spinal problems. As *Elixir*: For expansion of consciousness, especially in healers. Use a few drops in the bath to ease depression.

CALCITE

Location: Worldwide; exceptionally fine crystals from Iceland, UK and Czechoslovakia. *Hardness*: 3. *Specific Gravity*: 2.7. *Crystal System*: Hexagonal. Formed by the evaporation of calcium rich solutions. Usually colourless,

transparent, slightly milky pearl or pinkish-white. Clear
crystals were once used as prisms. Compact masses of
calcite such as lime and cement are used for building and
also in the manufacture of fertilisers and chemicals.
Properties: In healing, this stone assists in balancing the
male/female polarities. Reduces stress, grounds excess
energy and inspires a sense of lightness and joy. Some
claim it increases abilities in astral projection.

CELESTITE

Location: Finest quality crystals from Madagascar, England,
Tunisia, Sicily and Lake Erie (USA). *Hardness*: 3–3½.
Specific Gravity: 3.9. *Crystal System*: Orthorhombic. The
first celestite crystals found were a celestine blue, after
which they were named; other crystals are colourless or
white with bluish zones. The main source of strontium,
used to make signal flares and fireworks, its colour when
powdered and burned is bright crimson. Crystals are
translucent or transparent with a pearly lustre and are
slightly water soluble. *Properties*: Healing properties
include stress reduction and stimulation of thyroid
function. Brings peace of mind, clarity of thought and
speech and enhanced creative expression. Assists in
heightening awareness to finer vibrations.

CHALCEDONY

Group: Quartz. *Location*: India, Madagascar, Brazil and
Uruguay. Hardness: 6½–7. *Specific Gravity*: 2.58–2.64.
Crystal System: Hexagonal. A microcrystalline variety of
quartz, which usually forms fibrous masses. Most commonly
pale bluish grey, colours range from yellow to black.
Varieties include bloodstone, dark green spotted red — and
carnelian — brownish-orange to red. Natural crystals are

without layering or banding, although because they are porous they can be dyed. *Properties*: Bloodstone is a powerful physical healer. Oxygenates and strengthens the bloodstream, the heart, spleen and bone marrow and assists in balancing iron deficiency. Carnelian aids tissue regeneration and supports the functions of the kidneys, liver, lungs, pancreas and gall bladder. It is warming and vitalises the physical, emotional and mental bodies. As *Elixir*: Eases melancholy and touchiness. Brings objectivity and enthusiasm.

CITRINE

Group: Quartz. *Location*: Rare — some in Brazil, Madagascar, Russia, France and USA. *Hardness*: 7. *Specific Gravity*: 2.6. *Crystal System*: Hexagonal. Often used in imitation of topaz. Colour ranges from pure yellow to honey and brownish yellow and often banded like amethyst. A lot of commercial citrines are heat-treated amethysts or smoky quartz. When heated, citrine turns white and, if exposed to X-rays, dark brown. *Properties*: This 'drop of sunlight' brings hope and lifts the spirits. Raises self-esteem and enhances the body's healing energy. Good for digestive organs, colon, kidneys, liver and gall bladder, citrine assists detoxification. Also said to attract abundance to the wearer. As *Elixir*: Detoxifying and strengthening. Combats self-destructive thoughts and renews confidence in and connection with the higher self. Also used as atomiser.

DIAMOND

Location: Australia, South Africa, Russia, Arkansas (USA), Brazil, Venezuela, Ghana, Angola and Zaire. *Hardness*: 10. *Specific Gravity*: 3.5. *Crystal System*: Cubic. From the Greek *adamas*, meaning 'invincible', diamonds are formed in the depths of the earth, then blasted towards the surface by volcanic forces as pure crystallised carbon. Diamond seams run as deep as 200 km, so the surface is only scratched by mines that run to a depth of 1–2 km. The hardest of all crystals and this, combined with their brilliant sparkle (due to high refractivity), makes them uniquely desirable. Usually colourless, black, grey, brownish or green. Very rarely occur in colours such as blue, red, yellow or violet. *Properties*: Enhances brain function and is traditionally associated with strengthening the mind due to its hardness. It is a master healer, purifying the physical and etheric bodies and enhancing the full spectrum of energies in the whole being. Associated with abundance, purity, innocence and faithfulness and believed to be a powerful protection against negative thoughts. Some care should be taken, as the exceptionally strong energy radiated by diamond can overpower or drain personal energy.

EMERALD

Group: Beryl. *Location*: Colombia, India, Pakistan, Australia, Brazil, South Africa, Siberia, Tanzania, Zambia and Zimbabwe. *Hardness*: 7½–8. *Specific Gravity*: 2.6–2.8. *Crystal System*: Hexagonal. Has been valued through the ages as a precious stone. The deeper the green, the higher the value. Emeralds, which are very hard and prismatic, occur as crystals in granites and pegmatites close to an area of rising magma. They usually contain inclusions due to heating cracks, liquid or gas bubbles or to the presence of other crystals. Synthetic emeralds are now being made with artificial inclusions to simulate natural ones. *Properties*: Associated with Venus; growth, fertility and love. Vitalises and tones the body and mind, stimulating memory. Strengthens the heart, liver, kidneys and immune system. In the past, emeralds were used to heal skin problems and they

have a strong antiseptic reputation. They enhance dreams
and meditation and bring influences of prosperity, kindness,
tranquillity, patience and balance. As *Elixir*: Amplifies qualities
of kindness, patience and balance. Relieves hidden fears.

FLUORITE

Group: Halite. *Location*: Extremely widespread; fine
examples from many areas — USA, Canada, Mexico,
Germany, Norway, Sweden and Russia; also many areas
of the UK — Yorkshire Dales, Derbyshire Peaks (main
source of Blue John), the Mendips, Cumbria, North Wales
and Cornwall. *Hardness*: 4. *Specific Gravity*: 3.3. *Crystal
System*: Cubic. Cubic shape and octahedral cleavage is
distinctive. They form in hydrothermal mineral veins and
occur as transparent or in a great variety of colours
ranging from deep purple, pink and blue to green and
yellow, depending on the elements bound into the crystal
structure. An important component in the chemical
industry. *Properties*: Strengthens the teeth and bones and
assists in the absorption of nutrients. Especially useful if
worn close to tooth enamels, e.g. as earrings. The
influence is grounding, improving concentration and
meditation. Works with chakras according to colour.
Exposure to blue light amplifies properties. As *Elixir*: For
anxiety, stress and sexual frustration.

GARNET

Group: Garnet (the more common garnets are named and
distinguished by colour and other features). *Location*:
Widespread; notable examples from Switzerland, Austria,
Germany, Czechoslovakia, Italy, Russia, Finland, USA,
Canada, Mexico, Australia, Greenland, Tanzania and Kenya.
Hardness: 6½–7½. *Specific Gravity*: 3.5–4.3. *Crystal System*:

Cubic. Well formed trapezoid and rhomboid garnet crystals
are common, as are massive and granular formations.
Rhodolite is the most valuable of the red garnets and can
vary in colour from rose red to pale violet. Pyrope (from
the Greek *pyropos*, meaning 'fiery') is the deep red variety
of garnet and a semi-precious gemstone. Almandine is dark
brownish-red or purple-black — occasionally cut into
gemstones if very brightly coloured and clear. Spessartine is
yellowish-orange, to red-brown, and gem-quality stones are
rare. Grossular crystals of green or yellow tint often cut as
gemstones. Other forms include andradite and the
uncommon uvarovite. *Properties*: Red garnet is good for
strengthening the heart, thyroid, liver and kidneys.
Spessartine variety good for various types of anaemia.
Strongly associated with balancing the sex drive and the
potent forces of the kundalini. It spiritualises and uplifts,
improving interpersonal relationships and enhancing the
imagination. As *Elixir*: Eases nausea during detoxification.

HEMATITE (SPECULARITE)

Location: Main sources — Canada, USA, Brazil, Russia
and Angola; also UK, France, Italy, Switzerland, Austria
and Germany. *Hardness*: 5½–6½. *Specific Gravity*: 4.9–5.3.
Crystal System: Hexagonal. This heavy black, iron grey or
reddish crystal has a strong metallic lustre. Vivid red when
powdered. The principal source of iron ore, it is also used
in polishes and as a pigment. A fairly common
hydrothermal mineral, which forms under oxidising
conditions in igneous rock and in many sedimentary
rocks. Forms large replacement deposits as well. Popular in
Victorian mourning jewellery, it is still used in rings and
bead necklaces. *Properties*: Ancient Egyptians used hematite
to treat inflammations, haemorrhages and hysteria. Galen

used it for inflamed eyelids and headaches and Pliny for
blood and bilious disorders, burns and to heal wounds.
Energising and slightly grounding, good for the circulation
of oxygen in the blood and for stress resistance. It
strengthens the will, personal courage and optimism. As
Elixir: Treats low vitality and low self-esteem.

Jade

Location: China, Tibet, Burma, Japan, New Zealand,
Guatemala and USA. *Hardness*: 6½–7. *Specific Gravity*: 3.4.
Crystal System: Monoclinic. Was used for making
prehistoric weapons and tools because it does not splinter
easily. The name derives from the Spanish *piedra de ijada*,
meaning 'stone of the side', because it was believed jade
cured kidney problems if placed on the side of the body.
Although we associate jade with the Orient, it was valued
more highly than gold in pre-Columban cultures; carries
mystical associations to this day, despite good synthetics.
Rarely found in crystal form and more commonly as large
alluvial pebbles, it is usually green or greyish white;
occasionally found in blue-grey, lilac, yellow, orange, red
or brown. *Properties*: In China, jade was used to increase
longevity, strengthen the body and make men more fertile,
also to assist with childbirth and relieve eye disorders.
Associated with the five chief Chinese virtues of wisdom,
courage, justice, mercy and modesty. Jade has a nurturing
and peaceful quality, bringing healing and emotional
balance. As *Elixir*: Brings realism, integrity and assists in
ability to express true feelings.

Jasper

Group: Quartz. *Location*: Worldwide; famous deposits in
Germany, France, India, Russia and USA. *Hardness*: 6½–7.

Specific Gravity: 2.6–2.9. *Crystal System*: Hexagonal. Named from the Greek *iaspis*, the 'spotted stone', after the spotting on the green variety, Jasper is a form of chalcedony (see chalcedony: bloodstone). Single coloured jaspers are rare; range of colours varies but often red-brown. A yellow form is found in Mexico and USA. *Properties*: Healing properties include strengthening the physical body, especially the liver, bladder and gall bladder. Associated with the element of earth, it is physically and emotionally grounding. As *Elixir*: Helps those suffering from nightmares and disturbed dream states.

KUNZITE

Group: Spodumene. *Location*: Madagascar, Brazil and USA. *Hardness*: 6–7. *Specific Gravity*: 3.2. *Crystal System*: Monoclinic. Formed in granite pegmatites, this rose-pink or light violet crystal is named after the gemologist, George Frederick Kunz. Normally long and prismatic with uneven terminations; shows different depths of colour when viewed from different directions. Mined for its lithium content and also cut into gemstones. *Properties*: Lithium is used in medicine to treat a large range of illnesses from alcoholism to Parkinson's Disease and mental disorders. Useful in treating addictive behaviour and depressive conditions. It balances the cardiovascular system at a physical and cellular level and assists general tissue regeneration. Helps to increase the flow of life force into the physical body. The energy of this crystal is enhanced if placed under the colour red for about fifteen minutes. As *Elixir*: Assists in breaking addictive behaviour and in re-aligning the subtle bodies.

KYANITE

Location: Widespread; good examples from Brazil, Austria, Switzerland, France, Sri Lanka, India, Kenya, Australia and

USA. *Hardness*: 6–7 across cleavage planes, 4–5 along them. *Specific Gravity*: 3.6. *Crystal System*: Triclinic. Occurs in aluminium-rich metamorphic rock. Used industrially for making specialised high-temperature and acid-resistant porcelain products, as kyanite cannot be fused or dissolved in acid. Crystals are white, grey, light blue or greenish in colour, with perfect cleavage in two directions. *Properties*: Especially good for throat problems. Enhances the voice of singers and orators and generally benefits creative expression. Enhances qualities of loyalty, trust, devotion, reliability and serenity.

LABRADORITE

Group: Feldspar. *Location*: Very large specimens from Labrador (Canada); also Finland, Madagascar, Japan, Mexico and USA. *Hardness*: 6–6½. *Specific Gravity*: 2.6–2.75. *Crystal System*: Triclinic. Distinctive for its iridescent peacock blue, green and purple colours, which are displayed when the light strikes it, especially on a polished surface (probably due to light play on the twinned layers of the cleavage surface). It is a plagioclase, which is one of the essential minerals in igneous rocks. Used for decorative ornaments, small boxes, brooches, beads and other jewellery. Gets its name from Labrador, Canada. *Properties*: Beneficial to the nerves, brain, pineal and pituitary glands, the liver and the lymphatic system, it is also helpful in balancing and stabilising the movement of life force/sexual energy in the body. Enhances meditation and telepathy and increases inspiration, intuition, imagination and discernment. As *Elixir*: For unrealistic expectations and frustrated desires.

LAPIS LAZULI (LAZURITE)

Location: Afghanistan, Russia, Burma, Italy, Chile, Canada and USA. *Hardness*: 5–6. *Specific Gravity*: 2.4–2.9. *Crystal*

System: Cubic. The name derives from the Latin *lapis*, 'stone', and the Arabic *azul*, meaning 'blue'. This rich blue ornamental stone is often sprinkled with gold-coloured iron pyrites. In Medieval times it was powdered and used as a pigment similar to the 'ultramarine' pigment made today, but from synthetic stone. Lapis lazuli is a rare, usually massive, composite mineral found in marbles which are made by contact metamorphism.
Properties: In ancient times lapis lazuli was used to relieve ague, fever, blood disorders, eye problems, neuralgia and spasms. Good for enhancing psychic abilities, spiritual contact and for strengthening the skeletal system. As *Elixir*: Valuable detoxifier. For shy, introverted types. Helps self-expression and release of buried emotions.

MALACHITE

Location: Worldwide; large amounts from Zaire, Zambia, South Africa, Zimbabwe, Australia, Russia, USA and Israel. *Hardness*: 3½–4. *Specific Gravity*: 3.75–4. *Crystal System*: Monoclinic. A popular, green gem with a vitreous lustre — the name comes from the Greek *maloche*, because of its likeness to the leaves of the mallow plant — malachite is used as an ornamental stone which, when polished, displays its distinctive banding. It is usually formed in the upper, oxidization zone of copper deposits.
Properties: Traditionally used to strengthen the head, teeth, eyes, kidneys, pancreas, spleen and stomach. Also to promote sleep and increase fertility and lactation. Malachite was thought to protect the wearer from falling and avert faintness. This calming stone is a balancer to the physical and emotional system. As *Elixir*: Good protection against VDU radiation leakage. Inspires and re-balances burnt-out healers.

MOONSTONE (ADULARIA)

Group: Feldspar. *Location*: Australia, Burma, Sri Lanka, India, Tanzania and USA. *Hardness*: 6–6½. *Specific Gravity*: 2.6. *Crystal System*: Monoclinic. Named after its moon-like lustre, moonstone is a prized gem. It is a low temperature form of orthoclase common in many igneous rocks. Normally colourless with a pale grey or green tint, a silvery-white or blue shimmer and a mobile reflection. Star and cat's-eye moonstones are also found. *Properties*: Said to brighten at each new moon, the moonstone brings lunar qualities of psychic awareness, emotional sensitivity, peace and harmony. Long used as a protection against insanity, also to relieve stress and anxiety. Very good for all female ailments and for promoting general flexibility of attitudes. As *Elixir*: Good for those working out stress associated with the mother. Integrates emotions. Good for increasing sensitivity, care and attentiveness in those who tend to be overbearing or bossy.

OPAL

Group: Quartz. *Location*: Widespread, the finest from South Australia and New South Wales (Australia); also Mexico (particularly for fire opals), Guatemala, Honduras and USA. *Hardness*: 5½–6½. *Specific Gravity*: 1.9–2.5. *Crystal System*: No crystal system. From the Greek word *opalus* (from the Sanskrit *upala*, meaning 'precious stone'), opals were mined only in Czechoslovakia until the nineteenth century when they were found in Australia and America. They have no crystal structure, occurring amorphously in grape-like or stalactitic shapes within cavities and veins. Colour varies from milky pale blues and pinks to almost black. Extremely porous, and gem-quality opal displays a brilliant colour play probably due to optical light refraction among the closely packed balls of silica in its structure. Can contain as much as 30 per cent water by volume — very fragile. *Properties*: Historically, opals have been used to cure eye troubles and to improve vision. Their watery nature and sensitivity connects them with intuitive gifts and inspiration. Also have a reputation for assisting women in childbirth. Opals are stimulating to the pineal and pituitary glands and fine emotional balancers. As *Elixir*: Increases receptivity to new ideas and outside stimuli.

PERIDOT (OLIVINE)

Location: Widespread; large gem-quality stones from Burma, Sri Lanka, USA, Norway, Russia and Zebirget (Egypt), an island in the Red Sea. *Hardness*: 6½–7. *Specific Gravity*: 3.2–4.2. *Crystal System*: Orthorhombic. Usually olive or bottle green, yellow-green or brownish in colour and popular in jewellery. Olivine refers to the continuous series of crystals from fosterite to fayalite, of which peridot is the name for gem-quality fayalite. They form in igneous rocks rich in magnesium and iron. The properties of the crystal, specific gravity, fusing point etc., vary according to its iron content. *Properties*: Traditionally used to treat the liver and adrenals, to free the mind of envy and to create emotional stability. According to Rudolf Steiner, they activate physical and spiritual sight. Detoxifying and tissue regenerating, bringing increased vigour and enthusiasm to mind and body. As *Elixir*: Treats envy. Brings emotional relaxation.

QUARTZ

Group: Quartz. *Location*: Worldwide. One of the most common minerals making up the Earth's crust (12 per cent by volume). *Hardness*: 7. *Specific Gravity*: 2.65. *Crystal*

System: Hexagonal. The Greeks believed clear quartz was water frozen by the gods to remain ice forever and they named it *krustallos*, meaning 'ice'. Quartz crystals occur as six-sided prisms terminated by six triangular faces. Often twinned or in clusters and sometimes double terminated. There are many varieties of quartz, such as amethyst, rose or citrine (see separate entries) but this entry refers to the crystals commonly known as clear quartz or milky (snowy-white) quartz. Ranges within this category include rutilated quartz, containing acicular rutile inclusions which often look like beautiful golden hairs within the crystal; smoky quartz, smoky-grey or dark brown due to natural radiation (although much from the USA is artificially radiated to almost black); and herkimer diamond, found in Herkimer, New York State, formed in double terminated very clear crystals, somewhat like diamonds. *Properties*: **Clear quartz** is the 'universal healer'. Has long been believed to remove negative thoughts, increase psychism, enhance meditation and raise consciousness. It has been used in many cultures for healing and as a link with spiritual realms. Receives, stores, activates, amplifies and transmits energy, stimulating brain function and amplifying thought forms. As *Elixir*: For rigid, inflexible attitudes, emotional extremes and hysteria. All quartz is good protection against background radiation. **Milky quartz** is used in the same way as clear quartz, but is somewhat gentler and more diffuse, although a crystal's healing properties and potentials vary individually. **Rutilated quartz** is excellent for tissue regeneration, increasing the life force and for strengthening the immune system. Highly electric, very powerful and more intense than clear quartz. As *Elixir*: Boosts mental activity and eases depression. **Smoky quartz** is thought to increase fertility and balance sexual energy. Useful for clearing subconscious blocks and negativity at all levels, it is mildly sedative and good for easing depression. As *Elixir*: Use as atomiser to cleanse the aura. **Herkimer diamond** has similar qualities to clear quartz — it radiates energy, draws out toxins, releases stress and balances the energies of body and mind. Its radiance is enhanced if exposed to diamond. As *Elixir*: Especially valuable for relieving symptoms of stress.

RHODOCROSITE

Group: Calcite. *Location*: Fairly common; fine crystals from Colorado, USA, Mexico, Argentina, South Africa, Namibia, Rumania, Spain, Italy and Germany. *Hardness*: 3½–4½. *Specific Gravity*: 3.3–3.7. *Crystal System*: Hexagonal. Sometimes know as Inca-Rose, because it is found in stalactite formations in abandoned Inca silver mines, it is usually pale pink to deep rose-red in colour. Usually occurs in hydrothermal veins and sedimentary rock in massive or granular form, but occasionally as rhombohedral crystals with curved faces. The name is from the Greek *rhodon* meaning 'rose' and *chros*, 'colour'. In large quantities it is a source of manganese. *Properties*: Believed to help with emotional trauma and mental breakdown, increasing qualities of courage and will-power. Good for improving eyesight, treating spleen, kidney, heart and blood circulation, it also assists memory and aligns the subtle bodies. It balances passion with love, linking the solar plexus and the heart, and enhances self-esteem and acceptance. As *Elixir*: For emotional exhaustion and frustration.

RHODONITE

Location: Australia, New Zealand, Japan, Sweden, Italy, Russia, South Africa, USA and Brazil. *Hardness*: 5½–6½.

Specific Gravity: 3.4–3.7. *Crystal System*: Triclinic. Similar to Rhodochrosite, but harder, the most valuable rhodonite has black veins of manganese oxide running through its pink or reddish-brown crystals and is used as an ornamental stone. The normally massive or granular crystals are formed in manganese-rich metamorphosed limestones and hydrothermal veins. Unlike rhodochrosite, it is insoluble in acid. *Properties*: In healing, rhodonite is useful for physical and emotional trauma, to relieve anxiety and confusion, bringing a sense of calm and well-being. Good for the body reflexes, central nervous and immune systems, it is especially helpful for city dwellers, helping to balance sensitivity with strength. The rose and black variety aligns heart and root energies. As *Elixir*: For anxiety, confusion and emotional trauma. Promotes calm, confidence and self-worth.

ROSE QUARTZ

Group: Quartz. *Location*: Fairly common in its massive form; high quality crystals from USA, Brazil, Madagascar and Japan. *Hardness*: 7. *Specific Gravity*: 2.65. *Crystal System*: Hexagonal. The rose-pink colour of this crystal is caused by traces of titanium or manganese in the quartz. Its lovely colour makes it a prized ornamental stone, although it is somewhat brittle and difficult to work. Well-formed crystals are rare and flat-sided crystals were only found in Brazil in 1981. Tends to be milky rather than transparent and loses its colour when heated. *Properties*: Long associated with the heart and beauty, the 'love stone', is an excellent and gentle healer. Eases fear, guilt, jealousy, anger and resentment. A positive influence on the kidneys and the circulation, as well as increasing fertility, rose quartz is useful for blood disorders and most sexually-related illnesses. Very good for the skin and restoring a youthful complexion. Also said to offer protection against background radiation. As *Elixir*: Brings a life-enhancing awareness of beauty, self-responsibility and optimism. Rose quartz gem water as an atomiser or facewash is good for promoting clear, soft skin.

RUBY

Group: Corundum. *Location*: Burma, Afghanistan, India, Pakistan, Sri Lanka, Thailand, Africa, USA and China. *Hardness*: 9. *Specific Gravity*: 3.9–4.1. *Crystal System*: Hexagonal. Tend to occur in marble-like rocks, in some intermediate rocks and pegmatites. Rubies and sapphires are different colours of corundum, the crystalline form of aluminium oxide. Rubies, the red corundum, are much rarer than sapphires and have long been prized as the most precious coloured gemstone. Large gem-quality rubies are thirty to fifty times rarer than diamonds. Extremely hard, low-quality crystals are powdered and used for highly specialised cutting and polishing. Chrome causes their red colouring, often uneven in tone within the same deposit. They become darker when exposed to natural light and sometimes have tiny rutile inclusions giving the stones a silky appearance, which reflects light and can cause a six-pointed star effect. These rubies are cut as cabochons to show off the stars to perfection. Heat treatment is very commonly used to enhance the clarity and colour. *Properties*: The prince of gemstones, associated with leadership and authority. Traditionally used to preserve the body and improve the mind. Strengthens the blood, the heart and immunity, stimulates creativity and invigorates the entire physical and mental system. Ruby brings qualities of courage and integrity to leadership and power. As *Elixir*:

Balances heart chakra and amplifies energy of divine love. Helps those dealing with distress around the father relationship. Stops procrastination, bringing focus and confidence.

SAPPHIRE

Group: Corundum. *Location*: Montana (USA), Kashmir (India), Australia, Brazil, Burma, Cambodia, Thailand and Central and Eastern Africa. *Hardness*: 9. *Specific Gravity*: 3.9–4.1. *Crystal System*: Hexagonal. The name derives from the Greek *sapphirus*, meaning 'blue', although sapphires can also be violet, green, pink or yellow, depending on varying traces of iron, titanium, vanadium or chrome within the stone. Sapphires from Kashmir are characteristically pure, cornflower blue; those from Sri Lanka are patchy blue and Australian sapphires are deep blue with a greenish-blue reflection. Heat treatment is very common and is difficult to detect except in a magnified cross-section. *Properties*: Widely associated with truth and wisdom, the sapphire is thought to balance desire and passion with divine inspiration. The three points within a star sapphire are said to represent destiny, faith and hope, so this gem is particularly associated with granting wishes. Also good for the pituitary gland and, therefore, the whole glandular system, the heart and the kidneys. Associated with awakening psychic gifts and bringing inspiration and clarity to communication.

SELENITE (GYPSUM)

Location: UK, Russia, France, USA, Chile, Mexico, USA and Sicily; high quality clusters discovered in Madagascar in 1995. *Hardness*: 2. *Specific Gravity*: 2.35. *Crystal System*: Monoclinic. The clear, transparent form of gypsum. (Rosette shaped masses of gypsum with a lot of sand in them are called desert roses and the granular form is known as alabaster.) It is very soft and scratchable with a fingernail. The long, tabular crystals often display swallowtail twinning. Gypsum is used in the manufacture of plaster of Paris and for fine white plaster-work. The most common sulphate mineral, it is also a fertiliser and used in glass making. *Properties*: As the homeopathic remedy — calcarea sulphurica — it is used to treat mucous discharges, skin eruptions, glandular swelling and problems with the tongue. Selenite is good for strengthening teeth and bones and for restoring elasticity to the skin, tissue regeneration and rejuvenating the prostate, testicles and uterus. The energy is soothing and grounding.

SODALITE

Location: Brazil, Bolivia, Greenland, Russia, Burma, India, Canada, USA, Romania, Portugal, Italy and Norway. *Hardness*: 5½–6. *Specific Gravity*: 2.2. *Crystal System*: Cubic. Often confused with the less common lapis lazuli because of its blue colour and the fact that it can contain iron pyrites, sodalite forms in alkaline igneous rocks and silica-deficient lavas. Usually massive, from blue to violet and white to grey. The white patches are usually caused by calcite. Named for its sodium content, which makes it easily fusible. *Properties*: Believed to stimulate the thyroid and boost the metabolism generally, sodalite also aids the pancreas and the lymphatic system. The most 'grounded' of the indigo stones, it balances, calms and clears the mind, removing illusion and fear. Very good for those who are overly sensitive, it has similar qualities to those of lapis lazuli. As *Elixir*: Eases conflicts between conscious and subconscious impulses. Relieves fearfulness and guilt. Promotes courage and endurance.

TIGER'S EYE

Group: Quartz. *Location*: South Africa, Western Australia, Burma, India and USA. *Hardness*: 7. *Specific Gravity*: 2.6. *Crystal System*: Hexagonal (but micro-crystalline). A banded chalcedony quartz, it is formed with crocidolite fibres which give it its characteristic sheen. The distinctive stripes are golden to brown, caused by the brown iron content, against a nearly black ground. Often made into decorative objects. *Properties*: Good for the digestive system — the pancreas, liver, stomach, spleen and colon. Helps deal with 'butterflies in the tummy', bringing courage while softening stubborn pride. Strong but flexible, it enhances insight and clear perception, balancing and grounding personal power. As *Elixir*: Treats stage fright and fear of success.

TOPAZ

Location: Brazil, Germany, Italy, Japan, Afghanistan, Burma, Africa, USA, Ukraine and Russia. *Hardness*: 8. *Specific Gravity*: 3.6. *Crystal System*: Orthorhombic. Crystals of up to 270 kg have been found in Minas Gerais in Brazil. These hard, prismatic, granular or massive crystals are formed in pegmatites from very highly compressed magma. *Topas* means 'heat' or 'fire' in Sanskrit—possibly the origin of the word. A fine gemstone, true topaz is yellow, light to golden. There are three other varieties — pink, blue and colourless, although many colourless topazes are irradiated to make them blue; yellowish stones can be heat-treated to turn them pink. *Properties*: Said to bring the strength to deal with life's trials. Balances the emotions and calms the temper. It warms and awakens, bringing hopefulness and radiance. Strengthens and regenerates the cell tissues and is an excellent detoxifier. Also good for the thyroid, metabolism and digestive organs. This soothing stone assists all forms of creativity in harmony with the higher self. As *Elixir*: For anger, jealousy, worry and depression. Stabilises emotions and calms passions.

TOURMALINE

Location: Austria, Yugoslavia, Urals, Norway, Elba, Madagascar, Mozambique, Sri Lanka, Burma, Nepal, Brazil, Australia and USA. *Hardness*: 7. *Specific Gravity*: 2.9–3.2. *Crystal System*: Hexagonal. Occurs most commonly as very dark blue-green or black and this type is known as schorlite. Can also be pink, red, orange, green and colourless. The crystals usually occur as elongated prismatic columns, usually in granites or pegmatites, and are often zoned in different colours — green at the outside to pink or red at the centre is known as 'watermelon' tourmaline. Fine examples are often sliced and polished as ornaments. When heated or rubbed, tourmaline produces a positive and negative electromagnetic charge. *Properties*: Strengthening and vitalising to the body, tourmaline was traditionally used to calm the nerves, dispel fears, improve concentration, bring restful sleep, ease blood poisoning and infectious diseases and regulate hormones. Enhances the crystalline properties of the body, balances the subtle bodies and is strongly protective. Watermelon tourmaline is also good for balancing the endocrine system and metabolism. A powerful healer with highly electromagnetic properties. As *Elixir*: Excellent for treating negative conditions caused by geopathic stress and background radiation.

TURQUOISE

Location: Iran, Tibet, France, Chile and USA. *Hardness*:
5–6. *Specific Gravity*: 2.8. *Crystal System*: Triclinic. From
the French, meaning 'Turkish stone', historically turquoise
was often mined in Iran then came to Europe via Turkey
and so was thought to originate there. Sacred to the
Pueblo Indians of New Mexico. Usually opaque bright to
light blue or greenish blue, turquoise used not to be
thought crystalline until crystals were found in 1911 in
Virginia, USA. Normally found as massive or nodular
aggregates, it forms due to alterations in aluminium-rich
igneous and sedimentary rocks. *Properties*: Used in ancient
Egypt for cataracts and eye problems. It was thought to
strengthen work animals and to change colour to warn its
wearer of danger. Calming and peaceful. Its high copper
content makes it a fine energy conductor, vitalising the
blood, toning the body and assisting tissue regeneration.
As *Elixir*: Protects against environmental pollution.
Promotes efficient absorption of nutrients and general
healing.

Helpful Addresses

A stamped addressed envelope is appreciated with all inquiries.

Crystal Healing

IRELAND

Jacquie Burgess
Slaney House, Tullow, Co. Carlow.
Tel.: 0503 51057.

Also at:
Natural Health Clinic
The Mews, 157 Leinster Road, Rathmines, Dublin 6.
Tel.: 01 4961316.

UNITED KINGDOM

Academy of Crystal and Natural Healing
Highland Holistic Clinic and Study Centre, Craig Gowan,
Carrbridge, Invernesshire PH 33 3AX.
Tel.: 01479 841257.

Affiliation of Crystal Healing Organisations (ACHO)
46 Lower Green Road, Esher, Surrey KT10 8HD.
The ACHO maintains a practitioner register of qualified
crystal healers throughout Great Britain. All members are
required to comply with a code of conduct.

**Stephanie Collins, International College
of Crystal Healing**
46 Lower Green Road, Esher, Surrey KT10 8HD.

Cornwall School of Crystal Healing
Morden Farm, Callington, Cornwall.
Tel.: 01579 350783.

Kathleen Huddleston, Spiritual Venturers Association
72 Pasture Road, Goole, Humberside DN14.
Tel.: 01405 769119.

Institute of Crystal and Gem Therapists
2 Kerswell Cottages, Exmister, Exeter, Devon EX6 8AY.
Tel.: 01392 832005.

International Association of Crystal Healing Therapists
GAIA, Unit 19, The Corn Exchange, Manchester M4 3EY.
Tel.: 0161 7028191.

Geoffrey Keyte, Crystal 2000
37 Bromley Road, St Anne's-on-Sea, Lancashire RY8 1PQ.

Laurel Farm Clinic
17 Carlingcott, Peasedown, St John, Bath BA2 8AN.
Tel.: 01761 434098.

Harry Oldfield, School of Electro-Crystal Therapy
117 Long Drive, South Ruislip, Middlesex HA4 0HL.
Tel.: 0181 841 1716.

School of White Crystal Healing
4 Combe Hill, Combe St Nicholas, Somerset TA20 3AW.
Tel.: 01640 52346.

**Dennis West, Academy of Crystal
and Natural Awareness**
4 Bridgewater Road, Bleadon, Weston-Super Mare,
Avon BS24 0DG.

Healing

Confederation of Healing Organisations (CHO)
The Red and White House, 113 High Street,
Berkhamsted, Hertfordshire HP4 2DJ.

The CHO is a registered charity. It is a national confederation of fifteen independent and self-administering healing associations, representing over 6,000 healers — the largest complementary therapy group in the UK and with contacts in thirty-five countries overseas.

Dreams

The Dream Research Centre
8 Willow Road, London NW3.

Crystal Suppliers

Crystals are now widely available in New Age and natural health stores, as well as from mineral and lapidary suppliers. Listed below are just some of the numerous suppliers you may have access to — some are retail outlets, others are direct mail or both.

IRELAND

Crystal Connection
46 Sheares Street, Cork.

Crystal Mystique
Townyard Lane, Malahide, Co. Dublin.

The Natural Health Clinic
The Mews, 157 Leinster Road, Rathmines, Dublin 6.

The Natural Living Centre
Walmer House, Station Road, Raheny, Dublin 5.

George Peche
Garden Flat, 3 Belgrave Square, Dublin 2.

UNITED KINGDOM

Arcania
17 Union Passage, Bath Avon BA1 1RE.

Crystal and Gem Research Association
12 Cliff Boulevard, Kimberley,
Nottinghamshire NG16 2LB.

Crystallize
347 Portobello Road, London W11 5SA.

Everlasting Gems
46 Lower Green Road, Esher, Surrey KT10 8HD.

Manchester Minerals
Longsight Street, Heaton Norris, Stockport, Cheshire SK4.

Minerals & Lapidary
1 Shepherd's Business Park, Lenwade,
Norwich NR9 5SH.

Mineral Stones Ltd
98 Hatton Garden, London EC1N 8NX.

Moonstone
39 Church Road, Holywood, Co. Down,
Northern Ireland BT18 9BU.

Opie Gems
57 East Street, Ilminster, Somerset TA19 0AW.

Wessex Implex Ltd
Stonebridge Farmhouse, Breadsell Lane,
St Leonard's-on-Sea, Sussex TN38 8EB.

Mr Wood Fossils
5 Cowgate Head, Grassmarket, Edinburgh EH1 1JY.

Recommended Reading

Adams, Dr Mike, 'Crystal Antidotes to Power-Socket
  Radiation', in *Leading Edge*, Spring 1991.

Anderson, Mary, *Colour Healing*, Wellingborough:
  Aquarian Press 1979.

Bauer, Jaroslav and Bouska, Vladimir, *A Guide in Colour to
  Precious and Semiprecious Stones*.

Bonewitz, Ra, *Cosmic Crystals*, Wellingborough:
  Aquarian Press 1983.

Bonewitz, Ra, *The Cosmic Crystal Spiral*, Dorset:
  Element Books 1986.

Bowman, Catherine, *Crystal Awareness*, St Paul,
  Minnesota: Llewellyn Publications 1990.

Brennan, Barbara Ann, *Hands of Light*, New York:
  Bantam Books 1988.

British Museum, *Gemstones*, London:
  British Museum 1987.

Butler, W. E., *How to Read the Aura*, London:
  Aquarian Press 1971.

Caldecott, Moira, *Crystal Legends*, London:
  Aquarian Press.

Chase, Pamela and Pawlik, Jonathan, *The Newcastle Guide
  to Healing with Crystals* California: Newcastle 1988.

Chase, Pamela and Pawlik, Jonathan, *The Newcastle Guide
  to Healing with Gemstones*, California: Newcastle 1989.

Darling, Peter, *Crystal Identifier*, London: Apple Press 1991

Eliade, Mircea, *Shamanism*, London: Arkana 1989.

Gardner, Joy, *Color and Crystals, A Journey Through the
  Chakras*, California: Crossing Press 1988.

Goodwin, Matthew Oliver, *Numerology: The Complete
  Guide*, (3 volumes) California: Newcastle 1991.

Gurudas, *Gem Elixirs and Vibrational Healing*, (2 volumes)
    Colorado: Cassandra Press 1985, 1989.

Harner, Michael, *The Way of the Shaman*, New York:
    Bantam Books 1982.

Hunt, Roland, *The Seven Keys to Colour Healing*,
    Saffron Walden: C. W. Daniel 1971.

Kosminsky, Isidore, *The Magic and Science of Jewels and
    Stones*, California: Cassandra Press 1988.

Lansdowne, Zachary F., *The Chakras and Esoteric Healing*,
    Maine: Samuel Weiser 1986.

Mails, Thomas E., *Secret Native American Pathways*,
    Oklahoma: Council Oak Books 1995.

Melody, *Love is in the Earth*, (3 volumes) Colorado:
    Earth-Love Publishing 1993.

Mercer, Ian, *Crystals*, London: Natural History
    Museum.

Michell, John, *The View over Atlantis*, London:
    Abacus 1973.

Moore, Thomas, *Care of the Soul*, London: Piatkus 1992.

Ohashi, Wataru, *Do-It-Yourself Shiatsu*, London:
    Mandala 1977.

Palmer, Magda, *The Healing Power of Crystals*, London:
    Rider Books 1988.

Park, Glen, *The Art of Changing*, Bath: Ashgrove Press 1989.

Parkinson, Cornelia M., *Gem Magic* New York: Fawcett
    Columbine, Ballantine Books 1988.

Pellant, Chris, *Rocks, Minerals and Fossils of the World*,
    London: Pan Books 1990.

Pennicks, Nigel, *Sacred Geometry*, London: Turnstone.

Raphaell, Katrina, *Crystal Trilogy*, (3 volumes) Sante Fe:
    Aurora Press 1985, 1987, 1990.

Rinpoche, Sogyal, *The Tibetan Book of Living and Dying*,
    London: Rider Books 1992.

Sherwood, Keith, *Chakra Therapy*, Minnesota:
    Llewellyn 1991.

Smith, Michael G., *Crystal Power*, Minnesota:
    Llewellyn 1985.

Smith, Michael G., *Crystal Spirit*, Minnesota:
    Llewellyn 1990.

Spear, William, *Feng Shui Made Easy*, London:
    Thorsens 1995.

Sun Bear, Wabun Wind and Shawnodese, *Dreaming with
    the Wheel*, New York: Fireside, Simon & Schuster 1994.

Wombwell, Felicity, *The Goddess Changes*, London:
    Mandala 1991.

Index